Fatherless Sons

Healing the Legacy of Loss

Jonathan Diamond, Ph.D.

WILEY

John Wiley & Sons, Inc.

Published by John Wiley & Sons, Inc., Hoboken, New Jersey
Published simultaneously in Canada

Design and composition by Navta Associates, Inc.

For general information about our other products and services, please contact our Customer Care Department within the United States at (800) 762-2974, outside the United States at (317) 572-3993 or fax (317) 572-4002.

Wiley also publishes its books in a variety of electronic formats. Some content that appears in print may not be available in electronic books. For more information about Wiley products, visit our web site at www.wiley.com.

Library of Congress Cataloging-in-Publication Data:

Diamond, Jonathan, Ph. D.
  Fatherless sons : healing the legacy of loss / Jonathan Diamond.
    p. cm.
  "Published simultaneously in Canada."
  Includes bibliographical references and index.
  ISBN-13 978-0-471-21969-9 (cloth)
  ISBN-10 0-471-21969-X (cloth)
  1. Grief. 2. Fathers and sons. 3. Fathers—Death. 4. Loss (Psychology) I. Title.
  BF575.G7D52 2006
  155.9'37081—dc22

                                                            2006018002

Printed in the United States of America

10 9 8 7 6 5 4 3 2 1

Author's Note

The stories and events described in this book are drawn from my twenty years of practice as a psychotherapist. However, all the cases are composites. They have been deliberately altered in order to protect people's right to confidentiality and privacy.

In memory of my father,
Malcolm Luria Diamond,
and for my sons,
Julian and Oliver

It may be that when we no longer know what to do
we have come to our real work,
and that when we no longer know which way to go
we have come to our real journey.
The mind that is not baffled is not employed.
The impeded stream is the one that sings.

— WENDELL BERRY

Contents

Preface

This is a book about death, but it starts with a birth. My son Julian was born on June 17, 1997, at 11:01 on a Tuesday morning. The first person I wanted to share the news with was my father, so I called him from the delivery room. Dad was exuberant. He kept repeating, "That's wonderful news, just wonderful . . ." over and over, and then he cried.

There was joy inside Dad's tears, but there was also great sorrow. My father had waited his entire life to become a grandfather. When the moment finally arrived, he had little time left to enjoy it. He died six months and ten days later, his body ravaged by multiple myeloma, a form of bone cancer.

When my father died, some friends could not understand how I could miss someone in death who had been the source of so much pain and anguish when he was alive. They had witnessed how the contrast between my father's rageful and loving sides created more than an emotional crisis in my life—it was a spiritual state of emergency. They were the ones who helped me put myself together after yet another caustic, if not violent, run-in with the old man. However, it wasn't until he was diagnosed with cancer that real healing took place and the connection between my dad and me was transformed.

During one of my last visits with my father, I was sitting next to him while he held his grandson in his lap. After a few moments, Dad very tenderly put his hand on my head and left it there. "Does that mean I've done good?" I asked. "That means a lot of things," he replied.

Many friends called to ask me how I was and offered to help in any way possible. Three months after he died, people still asked how I was doing, but there was a hint of impatience in their voices—they were ready for me to start feeling better. After six months, they stopped asking altogether. After a year, most had pretty much forgotten about my loss.

It's been more than five years since my father died, and my relationship with him still has a hold on me. If time heals, it works in much larger increments: five years is a heartbeat.

Although my own clan and circle of friends grew tired of my mourning, people outside my circle shared their stories with me. Sometimes complete strangers would approach me at gatherings: "I heard you just lost your father. My dad passed away six months ago." "I was with my father when he died. It was the hardest thing I've ever done." When we dive beneath the particulars—cancer, abandonment, suicide, one year, two years, ten, twenty—we find our experiences are uncannily similar. Sometimes we even use the same language to describe them: "Our father was the glue that held the family together." "The old man was like a rock—he was always there with a hand when you needed it most." "My father was dead five years before I discovered how much I loved him." "I never knew my father, but when news of his death arrived it felt like a part of me had died too." "No one understood me like my father."

To begin naming and finding words for a pain that's unspeakable, for some, involves having to recall unthinkable acts of terror and betrayal. At times, mourning requires no less than

what the analyst Hans Loewald says psychotherapy requires—
that is, transforming the ghosts that haunt us into ancestors.

In all our myths and metaphors about dying, death isn't an
end, it's a passage. We talk of "crossing over" and speak of a person's "voyage" to the next world. This theme of travel shows up
as well in our dreams about death, in which we visit and receive
loved ones who are no longer with us.

There is an Aboriginal creation myth in which legendary
totemic beings wander over the continent in the Dreamtime,
singing out the name of everything that crosses their path—birds,
animals, plants, rocks, water holes—thereby singing the world into
existence. Over the course of time, these songlines become a
musical road map tracing the territorial spaces and paths that
people inhabit and share with the spirits of their ancestors. Indi-
viduals are born into one of the songlines but only know a section
of it. The way to extend one's knowledge of a particular songline
is to go on periodic "walkabouts" that lead to encounters with
others living far away who know of other melodies or parts.

Fatherless Sons represents my own walkabout of sorts. It is an
effort to come to terms with my father's death and the multitude
of feelings and territorial spaces I've inhabited in my grief.

In researching and writing this book, I wanted to get close to
sons' experiences of their fathers. This is a book about relationships, a collection of men's experiences with death, dying, deser-
tion, and I-Thou encounters with their fathers as well as their
own children. I've met many fellow travelers along the way, some
through my therapy practice and others who sought me out when
they heard I was researching this subject. Their stories gave me
hope.

Losing a father is one of the most profound events in a man's
life, and like the waves a stone causes when thrown into still
water, the ripples of loss continue on and on. This book is written
to help men understand how their past experiences continue to
affect their relationships with family and friends, lovers and

coworkers, and themselves. To those whose fathers are already gone, the book illuminates the possibility for a second chance—an opportunity for rediscovery—for men to feel compassion and forgiveness for their fathers and thereby free themselves from the emotional bonds that keep their present tied in knots, their future out of reach, and their past chained to a wounded soul.

Many of the stories collected here are a tribute to survival of abandonment, abuse, and neglect. However, even sons with mostly positive memories of their fathers must, as another writer observed, "endure the separation of death, the affliction of mourning."

Facing death takes great courage. No matter how confusing or painful a man's relationship with his father may have been, experiencing grief is heroic and sacred work. While the path you embarked on when you opened the book was about grieving, the journey is about healing.

Introduction

MY FATHER, MALCOLM DIAMOND, was a fixture at Princeton University for forty years. It was a mostly uphill ride from John Witherspoon Elementary School on Walnut Lane to my father's office in 1879 Hall, the medieval fortress that houses Princeton's religion department. It was hard work for my ten-year-old legs, and I always arrived out of breath. For me, fourth grade had started a week earlier, but it was my father's first day of classes. I climbed the spiral wooden staircase all the way to the top of the gothic spire of McCosh 50 and peered down from the balcony— the vantage point many students watched from. The auditorium, which held five hundred, was packed. No one noticed me enter; all eyes were fixed on my father. His brown tweed jacket with beige leather patches on both elbows was tossed on the floor behind him. The sleeves of his sweat-soaked white oxford dress shirt were rolled up, exposing his hairy forearms. A bright orange cotton tie hung loosely from his open collar.

Dad was just a speck on the stage, but his presence filled the hall. Ivy League decorum gave way to Hasidic delight, Talmudic contentiousness, and Borscht Belt comedy. His listeners were enthralled. At the closing lines of his lecture, you could hear your own heartbeat, so thoroughly had he seized everyone's attention. And then, spontaneous and prolonged applause. It is not unheard of for a professor to receive such an enthusiastic ovation at the conclusion of a course; my father would get one after his first class.

With a faculty roster that included names like Toni Morrison, John Nash, Elaine Pagels, Ruth Simmons, Cornel West, and Andrew Wiles, Malcolm Diamond was certainly not the most celebrated or well-known professor to pass through Princeton's hallowed halls during his tenure. Few would dispute he was its most beloved.

When asked what he did for a living, it was my father's habit to simply say, "I teach college." If pressed further, in a light-hearted reference to the movie *Goodbye, Mr. Chips*—the sentimental James Hilton tale of an all-boys school in England and the prim and proper professor who lives for its existence—he would answer, "I am Princeton's Mr. Chipsky."

My father wasn't well enough to travel the summer Julian was born, so six weeks later I took my son to meet his grandfather. During that visit Dad sat me down, along with his wife, Denise, to go over what sort of service and burial he wanted. Dad asked me to deliver his eulogy, as he had done for his father. I felt like one of his students negotiating a deadline for my final assignment. I remember that the juxtaposition of the two events—meeting his grandson and planning for his death—felt both surreal and natural at the same time.

Trips to the doctor or the hospital due to complications from his cancer or his medication had become a routine part of every visit with my father. A cold would quickly become flu, and flu became pneumonia without any warning, which immediately meant another trip to the hospital. The stays varied in length from a few days to a month.

During one of these stays, in a phone call from his hospital bed, my father got the Hanukkah prayers confused. He had sung those prayers for more than seventy years. Each evening at sundown during Hanukkah, I called his room and put Julian on the phone. The first night he cried because he never thought he would be singing them to his grandson. The third night he said them backward.

We had been planning to visit him after the holidays. The next day I received a call from Denise, asking if I could come sooner. Dad's condition had worsened. She was very upset because, against my father's wishes, his doctor had put him on a ventilator.

On the way down, I drove like the wind. I had made this trip from western Massachusetts to New Jersey hundreds of times in my life. Crossing over into Connecticut, past Hartford, down Route 91 to the Merritt Parkway, the Merritt to the Hutchinson Parkway, the Hutch to the Cross County Parkway, the Cross County to the Henry Hudson Drive. It was a clear night, so traveling over the George Washington Bridge on route 95, I could see the Empire State Building, the World Trade Center, and the Statue of Liberty—beacons of my childhood, lighting my way home.

I pulled up to the gray parking monolith adjacent to the hospital and took the elevator to the main floor. Up another set of elevators, I pressed "3" for Oncology. When the doors opened I stepped off, paused, quickly stepped back inside, and pressed the button next to the letters "ICU." I had never been to the Intensive Care Unit before. When the elevator opened to the basement, I hesitated so long that the doors almost closed on me again. I was turned around and surprised to discover the floor containing the hospital's most fragile patients located in the basement among all the plumbing, wiring, and building infrastructure.

When I walked into the room, I barely recognized the man in the bed. My father had always been a strikingly handsome and charismatic man, even when sick. Now there were wires and tubes connected to every part of his body. The breathing apparatus pumping air into his lungs caused his chest to slowly rise and sink over and over. His eyes were bulging from all the pain medication and anesthesia he'd received when they put him on the ventilator.

I gave my father a kiss and placed a picture of Julian on his pillow.

The first doctor I came in contact with was a resident on call, a very well-meaning woman who wanted to place a tube in my father's stomach so he could be fed in this semicomatose state. After considerable discussion, she agreed to abide by Dad's wishes not to take any extreme measures to prolong his life. "Your father and you appear to have talked a good deal about these matters," she concluded. I spoke by phone with my father's own doctor, who said he would arrange to have him taken off life support the following day.

Dad's nurse, Laura, saw Julian's picture and brought me photographs of her four-month-old. She and I sat at the foot of Dad's bed comparing stories about sleepless nights.

Dad had only a short window of consciousness the entire evening. Laura asked him to squeeze my hand if he knew his son Jonathan was here. He did. Then she asked him if he was cold or in pain. He shook his head no.

My father always said that one of the worst things he could imagine about dying was his family feeling obligated to keep some sort of a death watch over him, so I like to think that the relative quiet in which we sat together was comforting to him. I say relative because at four in the morning alarms and whistles sounded from the legion of machines that were monitoring his vital signs, bringing nurses from every direction. Mercifully, the nurses did not call the doctor right away, which avoided any further Talmudic debate over the fine points in my father's living will.

A few minutes later, at 4:10 in morning, one of the nurses said, "He's gone." Several of the staff bowed their heads in silent prayer. I tried to join them, but I could barely hear myself think. The doctor I had spoken to earlier arrived shortly, but neither she nor the nurses could figure out how to turn off the alarms, so we all stood silently around my father while the hospital's shofars announced his ascendance to the heavens.

It's odd the things we remember about the events surrounding a person's death. We don't remember days, we remember moments. The details of the events that led up to and followed my father's death are very foggy, but those last hours spent with him before he died are emblazoned on my mind. There was no white light or divine moment when he crossed over. It was all a bit chaotic, very real, and in many ways a fairly typical day with my father.

His Eulogy

The day before my father's memorial, I took a walk across the campus. Everywhere I looked I saw little slumped-over professors wearing Burberry trench coats, wool scarves, tweed hats, and thick-soled shoes. For the next three blocks I watched myself repeat the same futile march up to each one of them just to be sure it wasn't Dad. Did I say three blocks? I meant three years.

The service was held inside the same building in which my father had taught his last class. I climbed the twelve steps up to the podium. Seeking a brief respite from the sea of faces waiting for me to start, I gazed up at the balcony and spotted my father's ten-year-old step-grandson Jarret wading through a row of empty seats where no one would notice him hiding. I wanted to join him.

I tried to stay present and composed while delivering my remarks, but speaking about my relationship with my father caused me untold pain—the pain of all the words and images I chose to share, as well as those I chose not to.

Breakfast, Sunday morning. My father was eating, hurrying to get to the office. Dad demanded his toast. My mother turned from the other plates she was preparing, stepped into the dining area, and shouted, "You want your toast, here's your God-damned toast!" and hurled the side order over his head. Neither my brother nor I had ever seen my mother stand up to our father in this fashion. Whenever our father wanted something that wasn't on the table, he acted as if he was complaining about bad service at a restaurant, behavior we already found disturbing and even more upsetting when it was directed toward our mother. But throughout all the bullying tantrums we witnessed over the years, she always responded the same way, ignoring or placating him. This time was different. Her defiance gave us a vicarious thrill. You never talked back to Dad when he was in one of these moods. I threw my brother a knowing glance. Suddenly, my father rose from his chair, walked into the kitchen, picked up each plate of bacon and eggs my mother had prepared, and started smashing them down, one at a time, on the counter. Shards of glass and food flew everywhere. My brother and I cleared out fast. After my father left the house, I went back into the kitchen. My mother was crying.

I began picking up the pieces.

This and other incidents like it were faith-shattering. Although they weren't everyday occurrences, they happened often enough that the memory of the last one had not quite faded when the next episode occurred. And the terror of this or some other type of violence was part of daily existence, although on some days the fear was closer to the surface than on others.

I always wished my mother had left my father sooner, but I understood why that was such a hard thing for her to do. Dad was capable of great expressions of love. This is what made his rages so painful and hard to bear—they undid such good.

My stepmother knew about my father's abuse of my mother, but thought it would be different for them. That makes her a statistic; another victim of men's violence against women. She also thought she'd met her soul mate, someone who wanted the same things from life that she did. That makes her human. It's important to hold on to both perspectives.

I was more traumatized by my father's marriages than by his parenting. Dad spent a lot of time in therapy with me, trying to make what happened between us right. However, not until the very end, when he went to a batterers' group, was he willing to take responsibility for how he treated the women he loved, at which point it felt like too little too late.

After my father died, I felt great relief knowing that his violence died with him. I hoped that his death would bring all of us who were hurt by his anger (including him) some peace. These thoughts, like so many memories of my father, occupy my own dreamtime and helped me come to terms with both men my father was. Even though I didn't share the words in this particular stanza with the hundreds of people in attendance at his memorial service, I consider them part of the same songline.

Breaking the Silence

Speaking the truth of Dad's violence in this book has been an important way of mending our relationship, and very healing for me personally; but for others, particularly my father's former students and clients—the ones he saw in a small psychotherapy practice he hoped to retire to—the reality of some of the shocking events depicted may take a while to register. It will not fit with their memories of the encouraging and nurturing professor who loved and guided them, and it will, no doubt, bring unexpected and new grief.

At bedrock, the two guiding principles I drew from my father's life were sympathy and love. Dad had a tough time living up to these ideals as a husband and father. "We teach what we need to learn most," he used to say. However, he applied both generously as a teacher and a therapist, where he recognized that the task of healing others is the only true way of healing oneself. I believe telling this part of my father's story serves the same purpose—that is, to transform experiences and emotions of derision and shame into gifts I can share with others, many of whom, I imagine, have had to struggle with similar experiences with a parent or someone they love.

Interviewing other men who lost their fathers, writing their stories and trying to understand what they meant, while writing about my own father's death wasn't easy. Every conversation brought up some previously overlooked aspect of my own painful experience.

On the other hand, I found the process healing beyond all expectation. It wasn't simply the catharsis of releasing long-suppressed emotion, although that did happen. It was the act of storytelling itself; it was my listening to other men's experiences and, in the course of our conversations, their witnessing mine. It all made me think of the Eugene O'Neill lines, "Man is born broken. He lives by mending. The grace of God is the glue."

The kind of grace O'Neill speaks of is hard to come by, but that shouldn't stop us from trying. In this book you will find, set between the chapters, some reflections on my relationship with my own father. In her *Long Life*, Mary Oliver invites readers to think of her poems as "little alleluias." Poetry is her way of offering praise to the world, especially the parts she can't explain or that aren't easily understood. Similar to the way Oliver writes about her verse, the passages about my father are not trying to explain anything: "They just sit there on the page, and breathe."

What I miss most about my father are his hugs. When I was a small child, I used to crawl into bed with him after his morning exercise—Dad smelling like sweat and Icy Hot, me burrowing my whole self into the crook of his arm while he read the newspaper. I can still feel the intense heat his body threw off. Even his love cast a fiery warmth. When it was time for him to get up and get ready for work, he would engulf me in a bear hug that would leave me smelling like him for hours. Like his spirit, Dad's embrace didn't just hold me, it lifted me up. And I haven't yet resolved the fact that the most violent and the most loving touch I've ever known came at the hand of the same man.

PART ONE

MOURNING HAS BROKEN

I will never mistake my memory of my father for my knowledge of him. But I am his heir, not his historian.

—LEON WIESELTIER

1

How Men Grieve

It's so curious: one can resist tears and "behave" very well in the hardest hours of grief. But then someone makes you a friendly sign behind a window, or one notices that a flower that was in bud only yesterday has suddenly blossomed, or a letter slips from a drawer . . . and everything collapses.

—COLETTE

GRIEF IS NOT RATIONAL. We keep coming up with new names for it—"uncomplicated mourning," "abnormal grief reactions," "anticipatory grief," "failure to grieve," "closure," and so on—in foolhardy attempts to understand and domesticate it. In reality, grieving is a messy and unruly process that's never had any respect for labels or the fine clean lines delineating one phase of mourning from another. Grief simply refuses to stay in the appropriate spaces we designate for it.

Grief makes us crazy.

Models and theories about bereavement are, as a whole, more helpful to authors trying to write about grief than to those of us going through it. Whether these theories use a "task" model (where successful resolution or adjustment to the loss is gauged by the mourner's mastery and completion of specific emotional tasks) or a "stage" model (where healthy bereavement is determined by a person moving through a series of difficult but necessary feeling states), the problem with all these perspectives is that they take an evaluative stance in relation to people's mourning.

Reading these "grief maps," one gets the impression that if you're not experiencing exactly what you're supposed to when they say you're supposed to, you're doing something wrong.

The most well known of this type of approach is Elisabeth Kübler-Ross's groundbreaking work on the stages of mourning—*denial, anger, bargaining, depression,* and *acceptance*—that terminally ill patients and their families move through. Kübler-Ross's model is now utilized by therapists, clergy, and hospice workers everywhere. Similar to many Freudian and Jungian concepts, her ideas are so popular and widespread that they have worked their way into our everyday conversations as well as the professional lexicon about death and dying.

I have nothing against this sort of thinking or theorizing about the grieving process per se, especially if it helps people who are feeling confused or disoriented to gain a better understanding of what they're feeling and experiencing (and why). However, even Kübler-Ross made clear that she intended her stages of mourning to be used descriptively, not proscriptively.

The real problem with models is that most of our experiences don't fit neatly into them. And even when they do, many of us don't want to organize and categorize our most painful losses this way.

The Exception Is the Rule

A friend of mine, Carroll Stowe, wrote a story in which he described a beautiful memory of his father's touch:

The last time I was privileged to shake my father's hand was at the 1980 Heath Fair. I had no way of knowing I would never see him or shake his hand again. That last handshake from my dad was so firm and strong it would belie his eighty-three years, a hand not gnarled from hard work but strong, kind, and good from many years of selfless toil.

His father died of a heart attack the following day.

The first time I heard Carroll tell this story, he was helping me clear some brush in our lower field. We were standing next to his gray '84 Ford F150. Carroll looked like Father Time. He had a thick, silver-white beard and a full head of hair to match. His face betrayed his seventy years, but the way his eyes sparkled when he sat on a tractor or held a chain saw in his hands, he didn't look a day over fifty.

"Jonathan," he said in his gruff Yankee accent, his eyes misting over, "it's been twenty years since I last held my father's hand in mine, but when I imagine his firm grip and heat from his warm palm it feels more like ten seconds." And then he pulled his right hand out of his pocket and stared at it as if he were eyeing a museum piece or a restored part to one of his cherished antique Farmall tractors.

Addressing the topic of grief and time, Hope Edelman writes, "We're an impatient culture, accustomed to gratifying most of our needs quickly. Expecting grief to run a quick, predictable course has led us to overpathologize the process, viewing normal responses as indicators of serious distress."

But as Edelman poignantly comments, "If it takes nine months to bring a life into this world, what makes us think we can let go of someone in less?"

Grief minutes are like dog years, based on some artificial notion of time. My friend Carroll's story captures the timelessness and intimacy of mourning in a way no model ever could.

Referring to Carroll as "my friend" is akin to calling the Atlantic "my ocean." He was a prolific author, storyteller supreme, good neighbor, logger, snow-plowman, expert on farm machinery and animals, wagon-train master, and our town historian. In short, a Heathan treasure. Sadly, he died on August 18, 2005, the day before the opening of what would have been his seventy-third Heath Fair.

His tractor sat for three days at the entrance to the fairgrounds adorned with flowers and cards from grown men who as boys had been introduced to the ways of farming and their first tractor ride sitting on his lap. Their children, including my sons, Julian and Oliver, decorated it with drawings and pictures of moonlit hayrides taken with their moms and dads in the back of Carroll's wagon, just as their parents had done with their mothers and fathers before them.

Carroll kept alive our agricultural past with humor and with great feeling for what we have lost and with caution to hold on to what we value most: our sense of community, the rewards of hard work, and respect for our land and our fellow creatures. He was a man of deep faith. When he wasn't cursing God over a broken-down tractor sitting idle in a field of freshly baled hay, he could be found praying to God in church. He believed in heaven. If such a place exists, now that he's there, I'm not sure what he's up to. But I know that when he arrived, his father's outstretched hand was there to greet him.

Kübler-Ross cautioned against our approaching grief in a formulaic fashion because, as she was fond of saying, when it comes to understanding death and dying, "the exception is the rule." This is an important lesson to remember. When teaching, regardless of the topic, I often tell my students or trainees, "All my ideas and concepts when applied to your individual clients are lies."

Each time two people sit together, they're starting from

scratch. It is up to therapist and client to do their own theory building and research. This does not mean that when consoling the bereaved we ought never draw on prior experience. It simply entails our remembering that grief is expressed in a range of ways; and while there are stages of sorrow, no two people mourn identically.

When a Boy Loses a Father

If losing a parent is one of the most stressful life-cycle events an individual can face, losing a parent during childhood is catastrophic. However, without a forum for discussing his feelings, the fatherless son has little validation for the magnitude of his loss. Unlike the adult, who experiences parental loss with a relatively intact sense of self, a boy who loses his father during childhood or adolescence incorporates the loss into his personality, where it becomes a defining characteristic of his identity. From learning at an early age that close relationships can be impermanent, security ephemeral, and family capable of being redefined, the fatherless son develops adult insight while still a child but has only juvenile resources to help him cope.

A boy's journey from childhood to adulthood is also complicated by the loss. Boys identify strongly with their fathers. However, while most boys separate from their fathers during adolescence to create an individual identity, and then spend the later years trying to return as an autonomous adult, the fatherless son moves forward alone.

Chronological age is not the only factor by which to measure the depth of a son's emotional attachment to his father, nor is it the most reliable. An older child, an adolescent, even an adult who has been unable to make secure attachments to a mother, father, or parental figure will respond with frustration and rage when the person he counts on to attend to his needs is absent.

Usually, however, from the time a child is two, the death of a parent is accompanied by profound disappointment, a loss of self-esteem, and fantasies of abandonment. These emotional devastations are, according to Louise Kaplan, "compounded by attributions of fault and responsibility, good and evil, and other complexities of conscience which, in a young child's mind, are always reduced to 'Who is to blame?' 'Who is the bad one?' 'Who made Daddy disappear?'"

Early loss is a maturing experience, forcing a child to age faster than his peers. Children take on adult roles, such as planning funerals, taking responsibility for younger siblings, or caring for an ailing parent. Without a father or father figure to guide him, a son has to piece together a healthy male identity and self-image on his own. The most trying thing about the way young people grieve (for parents and children alike) is that it happens incrementally: they grieve as they grow. Every few years, children reprocess the death of a parent in ways that match their new-found stage of cognitive development.

The news that an adult lost his or her mother at an early age often renders people speechless. The experience of losing a father is different. Often the first question asked when someone discovers that an adult lost his or her father at an early age is, how did your mother provide for you? It's as if the most defining or horrifying aspect of the loss they can imagine is the economic challenges the family faced. Not to minimize the trauma of sudden financial hardship or change in social status, but my own experience as a therapist tells me that these are not the most scarring aspects of the experience for children.

Images of Fatherhood

Both men's and women's experiences of their fathers' absence in death are colored by the way they experienced their presence in life. If the archetypal figure of motherhood is of a person who was always there for us, the image of fatherhood has become one of a person who was always gone. Consequently, for many, the death of a father crushes any hope of ever getting to know the man. Their pain is often more about the loss of what could have been than the loss of what they had.

If there is a cultural resistance to mother loss—an entrenched psychological denial or taboo—with fathers, it's almost the opposite. Although it is just as traumatic, there is less indignation; we almost expect it. Many of us are used to our fathers' comings and goings. We grew accustomed to long periods of absence—actual and emotional— and their movement in and out of our lives. Life conditions us to accept this as simply the way things are. In a sense, our entire lives have prepared us to cope with our fathers' absence. So rather than allowing ourselves time to grieve, we simply walk away from the experience.

For men, this is not that different from how we cope with many of the traumas and significant losses in our lives. Women are socialized to talk about this kind of experience; they are often more attuned to their bodies, their feelings, and other people. When men are confronted with a challenging emotional experience or catastrophic loss, we are taught to fight or take flight. Like mountain climbers who get caught in a deadly storm during their descent on Everest, we are trained to leave the bodies and our relationships behind and focus all our resources on surviving.

Bertrand Russell said the fundamental defect of fathers is that they want their children to be a credit to them. So much of our experience of the loss is tied up in our fathers' hopes and expectations for us, both real and imagined.

A client, a twenty-five-year-old musician named Philip, came to see me shortly after his father died. "I loved my father but I never told him because I was afraid he wouldn't say it back," said Philip.

Many fathers become paralyzed or choked with emotion when trying to say the words "I love you." Most find other ways of saying them and expressing their affection for their sons. What became clear to me after only a short time spent talking with Philip was that he would have no way of knowing how his father felt about him, as the two never spoke much at all.

Philip's father was a successful surgeon. Philip looked up to his dad and always assumed his career choice of music over medicine had been the source of great disappointment to him. The two never discussed the matter, and his father never said anything to him to indicate he felt that way; it was just an impression Philip formed over time. Following his father's death, Philip's mother told him that the only request his father made for his funeral was that his son play music. Philip knew then how proud his father had been of him. "I just wish he had told me," he said.

While every man's story tells a different tale about the nature of his relationship with his father, all demonstrate the power of the father-son bond and the hold it has on us throughout our lives. Philip portrays a father-son relationship glowing with pride and admiration for each other but tainted by the sadness of undeclared emotion.

To one degree or another, we are all—sons, daughters, mothers, and fathers—in a state of abbreviated or interrupted mourning. To escape hurt and disappointment, our hearts remain closed and our minds stubbornly disconnect from our bodies. What's sad about disengaging from the world in this way is that we don't just avoid disappointment, we avoid love.

These stories are not unusual. Hundreds of men I've seen in therapy have similar untold stories of grief and depression they carry with them, feelings of despair that haunt them, which they cannot explain. Oftentimes, men say, these feelings show up during moments when they're supposed to be experiencing joy, such as the birth of a child, a promotion at work, a son's graduation or wedding, or some other celebration, and they can't tell you exactly why.

Time, they say, heals. Time also ambushes.

Grief is not like other emotions; we don't seek it out. It finds us. And when it does, for most men, it's no accident. A neighbor of mine had a ten-year-old nephew whose father had just died. When I asked him how his nephew was doing, he said that it was tough on him but he was impressed at how well the boy was holding up. He told me they had just come back from the funeral that morning and how proud he was of his nephew because he "never lost it." "The kid teared up a bit," my neighbor continued. "I thought he was going to lose it a couple of times, but he held it together. He's tough, just like his old man. He's going to be okay, that one."

I fumbled for something to say that might make the boy's tears more acceptable to his uncle. I told him that in my experience, it was good for children to cry at times like these, because then it doesn't come back up on them later. But it didn't matter what I said. The men in this family were simply trying as best they could to come to terms with the devastating loss they'd just suffered, and this boy, like most male children his age, knew what was expected of him. His feelings about his father's death, dutifully cast aside at the beginning of his young life, will not resurface until years later.

In the meantime, all his grief and sadness will remain tucked away inside him until one day, in the distant future, some other loved one will die, or a precious possession will be stolen, or some important ideal will be lost. It is then, as Louise Kaplan observes in her *No Voice Is Ever Wholly Lost*, that the man who lost his father in childhood becomes overwhelmed by the feelings and thoughts he was not allowed to feel or think when the trauma first struck. Nor does the later loss he comes face-to-face with have to be on the same scale as the earlier one in order to elicit a son's unfinished grief. Sometimes it can be as simple as a change in job responsibilities or as insignificant as a lost scarf.

That was the case for my client Philip. For months after his father's funeral, Philip had not allowed himself to cry. Almost a year later, he was looking through his father's desk. It had been mostly cleaned out by this time, but he came across some address labels with his father's name on them. When Philip couldn't remember what the middle initial in his father's name stood for, he burst into tears.

The heart can open in sadness as much as it does in joy.

Philip used his father the way Doris Lessing describes, as a recurring dream, to be entered into when needed. "My dad was always there for me to love and hate; but it occurs to me that I was not always there for my father," said Philip. In their hearts, the men I spoke with never wanted to be at odds with their fathers, but most felt, over the years, especially when they were younger, that their fathers gave them no choice.

For some sons, the more they learned about their fathers, the more they disapproved of them. These were the ones who said, "It was better for both of us that he died when he did." However, the more genuine truth is that each time one of these men thinks of his father, all he wishes for is that his dad were still alive.

Despite all the anguish my own father caused me, the words "my father" will always make me smile.

The Soul in Grief

An entry from a client's journal written shortly after his father's death reads:

The night my father died I don't know how long I cried,
but I cried until I was cried out. And then it was gone.

Where did it go? I asked. I felt like the room should be a foot deep in bile and thorns and the foulest muck, but it was all just gone. I felt like I could both fall right asleep and go out and save the world. It felt like a huge weight had been lifted from my heart. Maybe that's what dying feels like, too. Whatever suffering we're carrying goes into the light, leaving our hearts free to float all the way away. Maybe that's why we can never be completely free of pain and heartache while we're alive . . . maybe every heart needs at least some suffering, to bind us to earth and to each other.

Grief is profoundly important to the human condition. A man who cannot grieve cannot love. It takes great courage to, as Hamlet cries, unpack our hearts with words, and commit ourselves to another person when the only promise we can be sure about in life is death.

A commitment is a promise in the present to do something in the future that may not be in our best interest at that time or may cause us great pain. It's the sweet sorrow of a father who knows his young son is growing up to leave him. Or the mixed emotion of a grown son who knows that before he can truly become an adult he, in turn, must witness his father's departure.

Our capacity for such commitment is what makes us human. It's why we don't just despair but rejoice in mourning, because while grief in its bitterness marks an end, it is also praise to the one who is gone.

Grief is the celebration of commitment.

REFLECTION

———

Ketchup

My father worried about everything. He worried about worrying. Dad had reason to worry. Without intervention he could get himself into serious trouble; and in a cruel twist of fate, he lacked any common sense whatsoever. He was truly his own worst enemy. My father had the uncanny ability to turn worry into an experience. Just driving to the grocery store for a bottle of ketchup could turn into a life-threatening event.

Counting down to the drive, there was mission prep. Car keys? This could take up an entire afternoon. Wallet? "Mission control, we're experiencing some technical problems, we're going to need to stop the count." And then there was the drive itself. A few near-death experiences later, you'd pull up to your final destination, so grateful to arrive in one piece that you didn't even bother mentioning the odd bump, scrape, or swipe in the parking lot. Inside the market, things took on a sense of urgency: "Ketchup, ketchup, ketchup . . . " "Dad?" "Don't talk to me now! . . . Ketchup, ketchup, ketchup." "Dad?" "Not now, damn it!" "They have signs above the aisles now, they're down here under 'Mustard, Ketchup, Oils, and Vinegar.'" "Oh yeah, *hah*! Way to go, Jon. Good thinking. Here we go now."

The expenditure of energy necessary to complete the most mundane task was mind-boggling. And these reckless acts of daily living—awesome eruptions and displays that they were—were not the exception. As Lyndon Johnson used to comment about his opponents, "The man couldn't pour piss out of a boot if the directions were written on the heel."

Cicero says that to philosophize is nothing else but to pre-pare for death. Dad spent his career preparing for his. Every day he woke up, stared all his intense worries, anxieties, and fears in the eye, and with an intimidating look—the sort of game face perfected by NBA stars and other pro athletes—said, "Bring it on!" Every peaceful, unencumbered moment of presence in his life was actually a battle. A battle he fought with his lifelong obstinate tenacity.

It was something to witness.

2

Do You Know Why You're Wonderful?

LESSONS ON LOVE AND ACCEPTANCE

WHEN MY FATHER INVITED his students to grapple with questions about the meaning of life and what we are here for, he would often quote T. S. Eliot's "The Four Quartets":

> Hints and guesses,
> Hints followed by guesses; and the rest
> Is prayer, observance, discipline, thought and action.

Prayer, observance, discipline, thought, and action are the means through which we grow and find meaning. Twenty years' experience as a psychotherapist has taught me that mourning requires the same kind of discipline. We can't change the forces of time. We need acceptance. As time passes since his death, I've been very aware of the myriad ways that my father is slowly slipping away from me, and I don't like it. Acceptance has been hard to come by.

When we lose someone important to us, we tend to lose them in pieces rather than all at once. I already feel my relationship with my father transforming into my memories of him. Even though it was a more raw hurt, I preferred when everything felt as though it had happened yesterday. Memories no longer have smell, or the sound of his voice—all the intangibles that were him. Today, I must be content to feed my father-hunger by spending time with my own children. I'm more father than son now.

Acceptance is a very popular term today that is being bandied about in more ways than one can imagine. So what does acceptance mean in the context of death? Do we need to accept our loved one's death before we can properly mourn, the way addicts need to accept their powerlessness over their addictions before they can recover? The answer, according to the existential philosophers my father spent his career studying and teaching, is yes. These thinkers felt that in order to truly live, we need to confront our fears about dying and to accept the finality of death. But I'm not so sure.

I'm thinking of the way Eckhart Tolle invites us to notice what we observe when we walk through a forest that has not been tamed and interfered with by man:

> You will see not only abundant life all around you, but you will also encounter fallen trees and decaying trunks, rotting leaves and decomposing matter at every step. Wherever you look, you will find death as well as life.
>
> Upon closer scrutiny, however, you will discover that the decomposing tree trunk and rotting leaves not only give birth to new life, but are full of life themselves. Microorganisms are at work. Molecules rearranging themselves. So death isn't to be found anywhere. There is only the metamorphosis of life forms.

What lesson can we learn from this? Death is not the opposite of life. Life has no opposite. The opposite of death is birth. Life is eternal, concludes Tolle. What I especially like about this perspective is that death is not viewed as a disease, something that must be cured or prevented at all costs; death is simply another part of life.

Anyone who has witnessed a birth understands that a place to stay untouched by death does not exist. Death and birth are totally connected and interdependent. We spend much of our approximately hundred-year life span between the two events trying to avoid thinking about this fact, but we come here alone, and we have to leave here alone. At no time is this more apparent than the moment you witness your son or daughter take their first breath or your father or mother take their last.

I have no way of knowing whether Tolle is correct about life being eternal. I don't think existentialist philosophers have any better idea of what happens to us after we die. What makes most sense to me is the way all of these perspectives speak to the universality and inimitability of the experience.

Remembering Crash

Nick Connolly is a handsome man of Irish descent with electric blue eyes and sandy blond hair that's graying around his temples. The clinical director of a large human service agency, Nick is passionate about gardening. After a day of talking to people about their problems, he likes to spend time immersing his hands in the earth: "In the spring, at the end of the day, you should smell like dirt."

When Nick told me the story of his father's death, we were sitting on his patio enjoying an iced tea together, surrounded by the fruits of his labor. After pausing to soak up the sun and take in the scent of fresh flowers, I apologized to Nick for making him talk about such painful things on such a glorious day. But the ordinariness and simple beauty of the day made it easier for Nick to recall the events he was telling me about. Nick experienced the same kind of moment the morning he found out that his father's forever had come that day.

It was a gorgeous Tuesday in March. Nick was in the yard with his partner, Michael, and their adopted baby girl, Livia, was asleep in her bedroom. She was just three days old. They were grabbing a moment outside, trying to figure out how they were going to be fathers and still keep their garden up, when the phone rang.

It was Nick's sister-in-law, Peggy. Nick's father, Crash, had had a heart attack on the golf course and was refusing to have a procedure that would save his life. Crash had told them he wanted to die. She would call Nick as soon as she knew anything else.

Nick thought he was going to be sick. What did she mean that his father was dying? He was saying the words "He's dying, my father is dying" over and over when he was interrupted by a second call, this time from his brother.

A group of them were driving as fast as they could to where their father was, to try to talk him into having the operation that might give him some more time. Nick reassured himself that they would talk their father into having this operation and that his father was going to be okay. Then he went upstairs to pack.

Nick grabbed his best black suit, and a strange sensation came over him. He turned to Michael and said, "I'm packing for my father's funeral and he's not even dead yet."

As he headed out the door, he received a third phone call. His brothers said his father didn't have much time left. Nick decided to call the hospital directly and got his father's room.

Nick's father answered the phone. He's dying, Nick thought to himself, and he's still answering the phone. "Dad, you've got to do this. You've got to —" He didn't even know what the name of the procedure was. He paused, then finished the sentence: "You've got to have this operation. You've got to live." "I'm okay. I'm okay. I'm not afraid," his father said. "Good-bye. I'm sorry I didn't get to meet Livia." Nick began to cry. His father told him he loved him and hung up.

Crash's heart had literally exploded. Later his doctor told Nick that it had a hole inside it the size of a quarter. Then they discovered a virus invading his body through his bloodstream. It probably had been in his system for some time but was attacking him more aggressively in his weakened condition. The CT scans, ultrasounds, blood analysis, and multiple cultures the doctors ordered were all in vain, as the operation couldn't have saved him, even if Crash had consented to it.

The Embrace

After Nick got off the phone with his father, Michael took Livia across the street to the neighbors. The next thing Nick knew, Michael was holding him. Looking back, Nick said it was the only thing he remembered making a difference. When Nick shared this last bit of information with me, my heart went out to Michael. It reminded me of all my wife Dana's failed missions to provide me humanitarian aid and comfort after my father died.

Following the loss of a father, wives, girlfriends, lovers don't so much console their grieving partners as endure them. If a spouse hasn't lost a parent himself or herself, these exchanges become potentially more hazardous as their efforts to meet their partner's often impossible demands undergo even closer scrutiny. Making things tougher still is the fact that, frequently, these allies in healing have a separate relationship with the deceased and are going through their own mourning process. Granted, their loss may not be as primary or devastating as their partner's, but that doesn't diminish its importance.

In my case, Dana's connection to my father was profound. Having virtually no father present in her life, she was drawn to

Dad. She loved him, and he adored her and believed in her. Complicating matters further, by comparison with mine, their interactions were relatively conflict-free. As the months and years passed, it became easier for us to share our sorrow, but initially these differences in our experiences of my father were painful to discover and often resulted in Dana feeling her grief crowded out by mine, or my feeling intruded upon by hers.

After their long embrace, Michael and Nick retrieved their baby from the neighbors and began the nine-hour drive to Watertown. Nick sat in the backseat with Livia. While his daughter rested in her car seat next to him, memories of his father raced through his mind.

It was Nick's fifth birthday. He could still hear the cries and complaints groaning from the tires of his father's 1966 T-bird convertible as it roared into the driveway of their two-story cape. His father hopped out of the car holding a huge box in his arms. They never wrapped presents in his family, so Nick could see it plain as day. He couldn't remember a happier moment in his life. "Daddy, you got it, you got it!" he shouted. It was the most perfect thing he'd ever seen. He couldn't read yet, but he knew what the words on the side of the box said. And as he sat in the backseat of the car staring at his infant daughter sleeping next to him, Nick mouthed them to himself: "E-A-S-Y B-A-K-E O-V-E-N."

Even now, Nick remembered the sheer delight his father took in his son's joy and excitement. It was the happiest he'd ever seen his father—cheeks glowing, smile beaming, eyes brimming with pride. But it was an expression he couldn't remember seeing on his father's face that filled Nick's heart at that moment. Crash's face displayed no shame. None whatsoever. At five years old, Nick had no idea that he wasn't supposed to ask for an Easy Bake Oven, and nothing his father did or said gave him any indication he should feel otherwise.

Nick remembered how when he turned fourteen he asked his father in a philosophical way, "Dad, what do you know about boys who have had experiences with other boys? Is that normal?" And at twenty-two when, after he had been coming out to his father his whole life, he finally said the words.

It was a few days before Christmas. Nick, just home from college, arrived late at night. Everyone else had gone to bed. As was his custom, Nick's father stayed up to wait for him. His dad was by himself at the dining room table, having some scotch. The two sat together talking, catching up on things, when Crash said, "You know, your mother told me that you're gay." "I meant to tell you," said Nick. And then his father looked at him and said something that he had said to Nick and his brothers and sisters a hundred, two hundred, three hundred times: "You know you're wonderful?" And Nick was required to say, "Yes." And then his father said, "Do you know why you're wonderful?" And he was required to say nothing. And his father said, "Because you're you." For the next fifteen minutes Nick pressed his face against his father's barrel chest and cried, while his father just patted the top of his head and rubbed his hand and didn't say anything, his son's head resting gently on his heart. That's how Nick came out to his father. That's when he knew, he really knew that it was okay for him to be gay. And that his father truly loved him.

There was no epiphany or exchange of that sort between father and son the night of Nick's fifth birthday. All that mattered to Crash in that moment was that his son know how much he loved him. If there was any message his father gave him with the gift, it was this: "It's safe to be who you are, with me."

Suddenly, the cell phone rang in the car, snapping Nick back to the present. It was his sister-in-law again. It was about nine-thirty. They were somewhere on the New York State Thruway. And she said, "Nick, I just want to tell you that Crash died a few minutes ago."

Several hours after their conversation, Crash's heart had

gone into arrest, and as he had requested, no efforts were made to revive him. "Just remember I loved you all," were Sean Frances "Crash" Connolly's last words, and he spoke them with eight of his children assembled around him and a photograph of his son Nick staring at him from the dresser opposite his bed.

The Awakening

The day his father died is one date that you can now and forever quiz Nick on. I found this to be the case for the majority of men I spoke with. We may not always remember our child's birthday, our wedding anniversary, or who won the World Series that year, but I have yet to meet a man who has ever forgotten where he was or what he was doing the day that terrible history began.

When Crash was a child, baseball was his life. More important, it was something he did with his father. Every weekend, playing catch, chasing fly balls—it filled their spring days and summer evenings. He was drafted out of college and made it as far as trying out for the New York Yankees at their farm camp in Florida, but he wasn't asked to stay on. Crash used to tell his children, "I could have been a pro ball player—I lacked only two things, ability and desire."

Crash described his being cut by the Yankees as more of an awakening than a disappointment. For him, baseball had always been more about his love for his father than his love for the game. Nick wondered if his father's having spent so much time as a young adult trying to make his own dad happy, pretending to be someone he wasn't, had made Crash more sensitive to the dilemma Nick faced as a gay man.

One thing was clear. Crash's unconditional acceptance of Nick's sexual identity made it very difficult for Nick to confront Crash about Crash's drinking problem. Nick was six years sober when his father died. He and I shared a good laugh thinking about how much harder it was for his father to accept his son's not drinking than his son's being gay.

Nick once tried to broach the subject of drinking with his father, whose friends, Nick discovered later, had given him the nickname Crash because of all the cars he'd wrecked. It was before Nick quit. After listening to his son's concerns, Crash asked Nick if he was familiar with Dylan Thomas's definition of a drinking problem. Nick answered no. "An alcoholic is someone you don't like who drinks as much as you do," his father shot back defensively. Nick never brought it up again.

One reason I was so drawn to Nick's story is that, like many men, he, too, appeared to be recovering as much from his father's life as from his death.

Despite his difficulty with Nick's decision to abstain, from that day forward Crash always offered his son water or soda, never alcohol. It was a small gesture, but it meant so much to Nick. When Nick shared this with me, I reminded him of AA's expression that an addict is a person with a spiritual calling who shows up at the wrong address. "That describes my father to a T," said Nick excitedly. "He had such a huge heart."

Now sixteen years sober, Nick said that were his father still alive today, he feels they could have that conversation about drinking they weren't able to have then. "I know so much more about talking to people," he said wistfully.

Ultimately, Nick thinks his father wasn't able to handle knowing his son harbored the same kind of pain and low self-worth he did. Regardless of the explanation, psychological or genetic, Nick felt the idea that Crash was somehow responsible for passing on that kind of legacy to his son was too much for his father to bear.

The result was many late nights spent on the phone, or in his dad's backyard under the giant oak tree, listening to his father pour his heart out to him in a drunken stupor. Nick hated those conversations. Still, he could never bring himself to end them.

Underneath the alcohol and bravado, he knew that all his father really wanted was an opportunity to connect. And Nick felt he owed his dad that much.

Nick remembered thinking to himself at the time how relieved he was going to be the day he no longer had to come home to those drunken phone messages and late-night phone calls from his dad. Today, he would give anything to talk to his father in any state.

For many sons, the death of their father is both liberating and traumatizing. The experience of losing your father can be terrible, but going through it can actually be quite wonderful, too. It's hard to imagine how much real joy there is commingled with all this awfulness. The freedom experienced can be as simple as the relief that comes from seeing a person we love end their suffering, or our no longer having to take care of a convalescent, dependent on us for his every need. Or it can be as complex as discovering the compassion that has always eluded us for a man whose life provided us the best and the worst memories our heart has ever known.

From the standpoint of mourning, acceptance means just that, accepting both the love and the hate and, as clichéd as it sounds, learning to take the good with the bad—and more. It's actively seeking out the good parts. Accepting someone in death requires no less than what it took to accept them in life. It is, as Janis Abrahm Spring writes in *How Can I Forgive You? The Courage to Forgive, the Freedom Not To*, "a gutsy life-affirming response" to relationships. It means honoring the full sweep of your emotions, challenging false assumptions about what happened in your relationship with the deceased, and honestly looking at your own contribution to whatever problems you may have experienced together. And most of all, if the person hurt you during his lifetime, looking for his humanity and trying to see him apart from the offense.

The Burial

Two days after he arrived in Watertown, Nick buried his father.

His family walked from the funeral parlor to Holy Family Church, where Nick had been baptized and confirmed, had received his first Holy Communion, and had attended services until he left home for college. It was only two blocks, so they decided to have a processional.

Coming out of the funeral parlor, as they passed Holy Family Grammar where Nick had gone to school, he was transported back to his childhood. He was eleven years old. Three girls from his class were following him down the very same block shouting "Femme, faggot, fairy" the whole way. He never looked at them. He just kept walking. Their taunts didn't stop until he ducked inside a building. It was the public library. Sanctuary. Climbing up the front steps, he tried to look as if he'd been heading there the whole time.

Those were just some of Nick's thoughts as the three of them walked the two blocks to his father's funeral—two men together with their baby, in the small town in upstate New York where Nick had grown up and had lived so ashamed and afraid of being gay.

It was an overcast day. Suddenly, the sun broke through the clouds like water pouring through a sieve, casting hundreds of small rays of light on the ground and the streets below. One of them caught Michael, Livia, and Nick in its beam, giving the impression of a light shining down on them from the heavens, the way scenes from the Bible are portrayed in stained glass and murals in large cathedrals and small churches across Europe and North America.

You couldn't miss it. All of Nick's relatives saw them. And all the people in the town saw them. They were radiant.

Søren Kierkegaard said it requires moral courage to grieve, and it requires religious courage to rejoice. Grieving for his father,

Nick didn't know what hurt more: his joy or his sadness. What he did know was that walking down Main Street behind his father's casket carrying his child with his loving partner at his side, he felt like rejoicing.

Nick looked at Michael and the baby he was holding in his arms, and a happiness he had never experienced before washed over him. It was familiar in one respect: just as with his sadness, he could not plumb its depths or find its ends.

REFLECTION

Thanksgiving '97

I don't think it ever truly sank in for me that my father was dying until Thanksgiving 1997, my son Julian's first and Dad's last. I brought Julian into New York City to my uncle's apartment to surprise my father.

It had been years since I'd been to a Thanksgiving celebration in my uncle's home. When my parents divorced, it was a given that holidays would be spent with my mother's side of the family. My father never challenged the time we spent with my mother's clan, but he also desperately wanted us to be there when he made the pilgrimage from his house in Princeton to his brother's table one last time. By then his health was touch-and-go. Hours before he was expected to arrive, he still wasn't sure he could make it.

The look on his face when he saw me standing in the foyer with Julian was what, in my metaphoric shorthand, I call a "career moment." If I did nothing else in my life other than provide my father with that moment, that would be enough. In Judaism it's what's known as a mitzvah (a good deed and then some). My father's spirit soared that night. While others were surprised by my presence, Dad never asked me what I was doing there. He knew.

Julian squealed with delight as he rocked on his grandfather's unsteady lap. I was terrified he might grab the shunt protruding from my father's neck, but Dad seemed unconcerned, almost nonchalant about it. My father and my five-and-a-half-month-old son, although separated by more than seventy-two years, had more in common that night than any two people in the room. Neither of them had any time, for my father had lost his and my son hadn't acquired his yet.

3

Help Me to Remember You

LESSONS ON LOSS AND ABANDONMENT

> There can be no deep disappointment where there is not deep love.
>
> —MARTIN LUTHER KING JR.

MY CLIENT ERVIN, a sixteen-year-old biracial young man, said he felt his blackness disappearing the same way his father had vanished from his life when Ervin was just six months old.

In therapy, Ervin and I talked about the need for him to seek out more successful adult black men as role models to fill the void his father had left. This was an especially difficult task for Ervin, as it brought him face-to-face with his father's absence from his life. This fact, coupled with his desire to better understand himself and where he came from, haunted Ervin. Up to this point, Ervin had depended on everyone's voice but his own for what little insight he had into his past. He and I talked about his need to begin forming his own relationship to these events. I suggested he start this quest by writing a letter to his father. The following week Ervin handed me his letter:

Dear Dad,

You know who this is right? Yeah it's me. *Your son!* The child you had with that white woman. My name is Ervin Munroe. I am your son. I'm 6'2". Only about an inch or two shorter than you. I'm 16. *Do* you remember me? I got this picture of you holding me when I was a baby. You're looking at me, you seem proud. But I am looking somewhere else, far off into the distance. I knew I wasn't going to stay.

Why have you never tried to reach us? Do you even care? I don't know I'm part black. Really, I can't believe it. I play basketball, Dad, I listen to rap music, I watched Belly, but that's about as black as I can make myself feel. Where were you to tell me I was black? I think you should come see me play basketball. I'm good, really good. I do something great on the court, and I look in the stands and see all these fathers cheering for me. But you're not there so it doesn't matter.

Mom says you're a nobody, a failure, that you can't hold down a job, that you pee on yourself, that you hit her, that you threatened to kill her, that you hold a bible in one hand and a baseball bat in the other. C'mon I say. It can't be like that. Look at me! I play the saxophone like Coltrane, I play basketball like Jordan, I write like Jesse Jackson, I make music better than anything you've ever heard in your life, but you have never heard it. You haven't even heard me talk. I am your goddamn son, and you haven't even heard me talk yet. You should see me. I'm distinguished, I'm handsome. Mom tells me everyday. I've got straight teeth. My calf muscles are huge, which helps me jump high. I get good grades too. There is no possible way that I am not going to succeed in life. But you're not there. Oh what you are missing out on!

Dad. Daddy. Pops. Poppa. Father. All these words are foreign to me. I've waited so long for you Dad. I have waited so long to love you. Every man I see. Every male relationship I have is based on finding a replacement for you. I want your guidance, I want your knowledge, I want you to tell me how the world works, how I fit in, and how I will become great. I want to hug you so badly. I want to hug you and have your big body engulf me. I want to cry on your chest and feel safe, and know that nothing is going to touch me, absolutely nothing. I want you to say, I love you son, and push me hard to excel in future endeavors. I want you to see me do something really mediocre and then praise me as if I just recreated the world. I want that. All this I want, all this I will never have. It is too late to tuck me in bed at night. It is too late for me to come screaming into your room at two in the morning, positively sure that there are robbers outside my window.

I've been searching for you in all these places. In my musical creations, in my sporting endeavors, in my school work, in my writing, but I never found you. Every coach I've ever had has told me how I should reach you. Work harder on Defense, Hustle, Get Rebounds, Be A Leader. They call it winning. In order to reach you, I've got to win and play well. That's what they tell me. I believed them for so long, Dad. All the black people told me if I could dunk the ball I could reach you. If I could jump and touch the top of the basket, the top of the world, that I could reach you.

When I find you, Dad, I will take you in my arms and cry on you. Whether you like it or not. I am going to lift weights, get strong, and grow three more inches so that when I take you in my arms and cry on you, you won't be able to get away.

Help me to remember you.

Ervin's correspondence left me speechless. Sometimes all therapy can offer people is a quiet witnessing; this seemed one of those times.

The two of us sat in silence. I held his letter in one hand and wiped away a tear with the other. Ervin waited patiently for a response, but the only sound I seemed capable of uttering was a raspy "Amen," which seemed appropriate, as Ervin's words read like a prayer. I remember thinking how remarkable they were to have come from the pen of such a young author.

Aspects of Ervin's story are unique to his experience as a biracial man of African American descent; however, many of the questions Ervin's letter poses strike a universal chord as well. How do we rescue our fathers from the trappings of despair, mental illness, poverty, oppression, abuse, consumerism, success, their own fathers, and most of all, themselves? How do our fathers want to be remembered? And, as Ervin pleaded with his own dad, how do we help them to remember us?

The father who abandons his son leaves behind an additional set of concerns. Whenever the loss of a father occurs with an accompanying feeling of abandonment—either physical or emotional—the impact on the son can be quite different from the loss of a father who was present in a man's life. The result can be heightened feelings of anger as well as extreme longing for what might have been.

According to the author Jon Katz, "Boys who grow up estranged from their fathers enter the world with particular disabilities." Katz's memoir, *Running to the Mountain*, is a witty and insightful midlife adventure, but it is also a painful chronicle of male abandonment and neglect. "Boys like me," confesses Katz—who has many skills and gifts that society doesn't typically value or recognize in men (e.g., writing, gardening, cooking, and childrearing)—"don't know how to do a lot of things. . . . How to tie a necktie, how to polish dress shoes, pack a suitcase, swing a bat, use tools, tell the difference between a Phillips screwdriver and the other kind." In one sense, these men are doomed, says Katz, as "to break with your father means you will never really have peace, never completely come to terms with who you are."

While I don't necessarily share Katz's pessimism about their prospects for moving on with their lives, I agree that men who grow up with serious, unresolved problems with their fathers encounter more difficulty than the rest of us. They may have trouble with authority. They may abhor shouting and screaming, or they may mostly communicate that way. They may have difficulty demonstrating compassion and empathy for others or expressing other strong emotions, particularly ones that result in their feeling vulnerable and dependent upon other people. They're often uncomfortable with other men and, because no one was there to teach them, experience confusion about what it is they're supposed to know. Unfortunately, for an angry and conflicted son, his father's death doesn't resolve these struggles; it complicates them.

As a young child, Ervin exhibited some of the traits Katz spoke of when describing boys with estranged or absent fathers. He bullied his classmates at school and was defiant and oppositional with his mother and teachers. I remember the day we met. Sitting on my couch holding one of my "stuffed" colleagues (a puppet wizard), Ervin didn't seem like the little tyrant his mother described on the phone. In fact, there was nothing little about him. Exceptionally tall for his age, Ervin was already playing basketball on the national stage as part of a traveling team of all-star eight- and nine-year-olds.

Ervin's mother, Dorothy, reported that Ervin's trouble at school coincided with his wanting to know more about his father and asking her lots of questions about the man. Dorothy wanted to respond to Ervin's inquires, but didn't know how many details of her abusive marriage and painful breakup were appropriate to share with her young son. On the other hand, she was concerned that Ervin was becoming alienated from his African American heritage, and so she tried to stay in contact with Ervin's relatives on his father's side of the family and chose schools that valued diversity and multicultural curriculums.

I brought a basketball to my second session with Ervin, and we played outdoors for our first and last time. Afterward, I swore I would never subject myself to that kind of embarrassment again. So the following week we moved inside to the Nerf ball court in my consulting room to play games of "p-i-g" and "h-o-r-s-e," where I at least had a chance of getting a basket. This strategy kept the scores a little closer, but rarely changed the outcome.

In fact, one could sum up my first treatment with Ervin as my simply allowing him to humiliate me in this fashion over and over. If nothing else, it gave me some insight into how Ervin was feeling about his own life at the time. After a year, I think Ervin came to the conclusion that if I could endure that kind of psychological punishment on our makeshift court without complaint, he could tolerate whatever shame he felt about the circumstances surrounding his father's absence and his secret wish to meet him someday.

Disorders of the Heart

After his marriage broke up, my client David began drinking a lot. He described bouts of intense sadness and fear that seemingly sprang from nowhere, and he complained of a loss of all feeling, a numbness that had infected all his relationships. He had difficulty concentrating at work and was missing deadlines, and his usually strong libido, which had often led him into trouble, seemed to have evaporated overnight. He wasn't attracted to people in the streets or people he had known and loved.

He thought he was losing himself. It scared him so much, he forced himself to have sex. It didn't work. His ex-wife and the few partners whom he had intimate relations with after their breakup complained that he seemed absent, somewhere else. He wasn't surprised. Whenever he found himself in sexual situations, his mind kept drifting off to shopping lists and work he needed to do. His friends grew worried and encouraged him to get help. He tried men's groups and Parents Without Partners, and he went to see several therapists on his own, but nothing seemed to help. In the meantime, he missed his son terribly.

Sitting in my office, his face buried in his hands, David was bereft. At forty, he hadn't planned on being the divorced, single father of a strapping thirteen-year-old boy, but that's what happened. David had the face of a proud, pained soldier torn from his home and sent out into the world for reasons he never fully understood.

It had been two years since he and his wife separated, he explained, and his son Andrew was about to turn fifteen. David was happiest when he was with his son. He felt strengthened by his presence. The two spent every other weekend and most school vacations together, but it wasn't the same as living under the same roof. Being a dad was the only part of David's life that offered him respite from his depression, and now it was only available to him on a part-time basis.

When I asked David about his relationship with his own father, he said his dad died when he was a teenager and that he missed him terribly. David described his father as the kind of man who wasn't just well liked, but was loved by everyone in town: "If there was a job to be done that no one was willing to take on, Dad would step up. He was forever volunteering his time on this or that committee. He coached Little League and belonged to both the Lions Club and the Masons. He had a big family and all these people who loved him. He was always in high spirits but he never felt happy." David delivered this last sentence the way an atheist might recite religious prayers on the Sabbath or grace before eating, like it wasn't important whether he believed what he was saying; it was only the ritual that mattered.

"The truth is," confessed David, "our father would fall into these dark moods and stay in his room for days on end. Our mother was at a loss. She didn't know what to do. My brothers and sisters and I would take turns trying to talk to him and make him feel better, but nothing any of us said ever helped."

When I asked him how his father died, David took a breath and held it. "He killed himself," he said, exhaling. "He hung himself from a beam in the basement of our home." David paused to take another breath. "I was the one who found him. It was right after I came home from school." I nodded numbly as I tried to absorb the image of his father's neck hanging from the noose. Then I sat, in shock, as David, in a very matter-of-fact manner, reported how he cut his father down, called 911, and tried to resuscitate him using CPR, until the paramedics arrived. His father was pronounced dead at the hospital.

"Everything stopped," is all David recalled about the period following his father's death. Everyone in the family was lost. David remembers feeling as if he couldn't move. A profound inertia came over him. It settled deep in his bones, and like a debilitating arthritis, still aches on days when the cold winds of this terrible memory return.

David hadn't shared this part of his story with any of the other therapists he had met with. He didn't see any connection between those events and the feelings he was experiencing now. "They happened so long ago," he said, perplexed and annoyed with me for intimating one. "How old was your father when he killed himself?" I asked.

"I had just turned fifteen," answered David.

The Impossible Subject

Whenever David thought about his father, his mind went automatically to the horrific circumstances of his father's death. This is an experience shared by many men mourning a father who has been killed or died in traumatic fashion, and it interferes with one of the primary goals of grieving, which is to positively reminisce.

If death provides a sense of finality or closure that abandonment does not, when a parent commits suicide it provides a tenuous one at best. I talked to a number of men who had fathers die this way during their childhoods, and the overriding feeling these young sons experienced growing up without fathers wasn't loss, it was abandonment.

At the time David came to see me, my father had been dead a year. Nonetheless, when helping him unpack his loss, I felt as if we were natives of the same country who spoke different dialects. Even though I had recently lost a father myself, I felt handicapped. I couldn't imagine losing a parent the way he had.

David seemed to confirm my feelings when he told me that from that awful point on, everywhere he went, he felt that people were staring at him. It was as if they could tell his father had killed himself and that the emotional scars he still bore inside were visible to all. Like all sudden deaths, suicide teaches us that relationships are unsafe and temporary and liable to end anytime, an awareness that can, for children, dramatically shape their emerging personalities.

"If psychoanalysis is the impossible profession, suicide is the impossible subject," writes the author Andrew Solomon. Suicide is a destructive act, and one of the first things demolished in its wake is understanding. "Why did he do it?" and "How could he do it?" are questions cast like a spell or hex on everything and everyone who had even the tiniest connection with the deceased. Understanding is the first step to acceptance, and only with acceptance can there be recovery. Suicide robs those left behind of this kind of understanding. Acceptance, if it is to be found at all, must be discovered some other way.

Gerald Schamess, a professor of social work and a colleague of mine with a long and distinguished career, has given this subject a lot of thought. Gerry's father was of another generation than David's. After losing a great deal of money in the stock market in 1929, with the help of his father-in-law he started a tire business. He was very successful at it, which allowed him to provide a comfortable life for Gerry and his mother and several relatives he employed. All this required him working long, hard hours. Growing up, Gerry rarely saw his dad. His fondest memory of his father is of a Sunday afternoon when they took a walk together, just the two of them, father and son, walking side-by-side holding hands.

Gerry's father killed himself when Gerry was only twelve years old. Gerry has only scattered memories of his father's death. The whole period of time is obscured by a thick haze that has never quite lifted.

Gerry told me the story while we sat in his office surrounded by stacks of articles and papers, his computer screen staring blankly at us from its perch on his oversized metallic desk: "He did it by jumping off the roof of an apartment house. We lived next door to a school, so he committed suicide sometime after three o'clock. A whole bunch of us were out in the schoolyard, running to see what had happened. I remember looking at the body, which was covered by a sheet or a blanket, seeing the shoes sticking out and thinking, those are my father's shoes."

A friend standing next to him seemed to read Gerry's mind. The boy put his hand on Gerry's shoulder and said, "It's not him, come on, let's go." His friend's compassionate response gave Gerry more time to absorb the terrible shock and prepare himself for the awful news that would greet him several hours later when he returned home.

As best Gerry can piece together, his father was very conflicted, though not a particularly unhappy person. Adding his
voice to the author Andrew Solomon's, Gerry said: "Killing oneself is a destructive act. It is rage turned against oneself in order
to keep from turning it against someone else. I know there are
other formulations, but that has always seemed right to me based
on my experience."

I appreciate the way Gerry softens his theory by casting it in
a relational light. In this sense, suicide is both a destructive act
and a protective one. Despite how it may appear to outside
observers or to those left behind to suffer its aftermath, suicide is
rarely a selfish act or an act of vengeance. This idea makes a great
deal of sense when the person is facing a life-threatening illness
or the prospect of a prolonged, painful death.

However, even though understanding is more easily achieved
under these conditions—"He didn't want to put him or us
through all that"—it doesn't make it any less painful. Needless to
say, when there are no such mitigating circumstances, the person's
actions are more confusing and harder to accept. Knowing that a
father, full of rage and self-loathing, may, unconsciously, have
taken his own life to protect his children and other family members from his destructive feelings offers little comfort to a grief-
stricken son. My sense is that given the choice, most sons who
have had to cope with life without their father would have preferred to take their chances.

Welcome This Pain

"Welcome this pain," wrote Ovid, "for you will learn from it." Or
as a colleague of mine, Roget Lockard, puts it: "Pain is inevitable;
the only pain we can avoid is the pain of trying to avoid pain."
David was an emotional survivor and a relatively successful one,
until his son approached the same age David was when his father

killed himself. At that point, instead of working from the inside out, David began using alcohol to heal himself from the outside in. By turning away from his grief, David wasn't just avoiding pain, he was avoiding recovery and the opportunities for healing that mourning provides.

For David, the catastrophe of his father's suicide was not only the loss of his dad but the loss of a chance to persuade his father to act differently, the loss of the chance to connect. Perhaps the single most difficult thing for David to accept was how much help and good information he was benefiting from that his father didn't have access to or chose not to take advantage of; and the constant wondering whether it would have been enough to make a difference if he had.

While acknowledging that his father's depression could have been worse than his, David said that what he misses most is not having his dad to talk about it with. In one of our sessions, David said he felt he had inherited all his father's "unfinished business." When I asked him to say what that meant to him, David responded, "I think he thought it would make things easier on us if he wasn't around, but he was wrong. I know it would devastate him to know that I struggle with the same feelings of despair and self-loathing. I'm sure he thought he took them with him. But the problems didn't leave or go away. Only he did."

The connection between grief and depression is complex, and their differences myriad. In his *The Noonday Demon: An Atlas of Depression*, Solomon covers this vast acreage with artistry, skill, compassion, and empathy. "Grief is depression in proportion to circumstances," writes Solomon, "depression is grief out of proportion to circumstance." David was experiencing plenty of both.

In our therapy together, I tried to bridge the gap between his father's world and his. I saw this as part of a larger project to recruit his father as an ally in David's battle with his own depressive moods. Toward this end, I asked David to think about an activity he missed doing with his own father that he might invite his son to join him in. "I used to love to do woodworking with him," he responded.

David still possessed his father's table saw, but since his divorce had no place to put it or any of the other tools he had inherited from his father. He described a small outbuilding on the property he was renting, which would make a nice shop. His landlord said he could do as he pleased with it. I suggested David not put this project off any longer.

This was not a random recommendation on my part, or something I "intuited" from my work with David. The author Tom Golden in his explorations of the differences between how men and women mourn found that men rely on activity and women on feelings to help them grieve. Golden noticed that as more and more of the tasks surrounding dying (e.g., building the coffin, digging the grave) have been subcontracted to the "death professionals," men in particular have lost many of the rituals and activities that used to provide them with a sense of meaning and purpose when faced with traumatic loss.

When his own father died suddenly in 1994, Golden began building a container for his father's ashes in his garage. He discovered that it was easier for him to connect with his grief through an "activity" rather than by simply "sharing" it. Many of his own and his father's male friends joined him in the workshop, telling stories about their relationship with his father. The workshop provided the men a safe place, a "container" for their emotions, while for women, he noticed, it was just the opposite. The women mourning his father's passing appeared to have great skill in simply sharing their grief. They were more drawn to connecting their pain, tears, and sorrow on a verbal level with their most intimate friends and family.

David asked his son to help him with his project, and when they finished, he was astonished to discover that the room they had built was almost an exact replica of his father's work space. David found this activity an incredibly gratifying and healing experience.

More rewarding than the project itself, which lifted David's spirits immensely, was the time spent working side by side with his son. In the course of putting the shop together, David said, he and his son talked more about the circumstances surrounding his father's death than the two of them ever had. His son was genuinely interested in hearing stories about his grandfather and was even more interested in learning about the kind of connection David enjoyed with him.

During one of our sessions, David asked me about my own father and whether he was still alive. I'm not sure why, but I found myself disclosing more details about that relationship to David than I had to any client prior. The harsh circumstances surrounding his own loss may have had something to do with it. I suppose I felt there was little I could say that would shock him.

David seemed amused when I suggested that it must have been harder for him to live with his loss. "I don't know, Jonathan," he said, gazing out the window at the maple tree outside my office. "Your dad sounds like a pretty complicated guy. In some ways, I imagine the memories of the man are much easier to live with than was the person. In my case, it was my father's death rather than his life I found traumatizing. He was one of the most gentle people I've ever known."

I was moved and humbled by David's insight. I felt embarrassed by my earlier thoughts about the horror of his grief and my focus on what separated us. When I looked at David, suddenly, in that moment, I felt we were just two sad, lonely sons missing their dads.

Not every son who has had to endure his father's suicide shares David's feelings about the experience. Nonetheless, his remarks made me realize just how ridiculous it is to try to create a hierarchy of loss within the realm of fathers.

Who suffered more? Such a question is absurd. The simple truth might be to say that every loss is unique. "When it comes to our societal understanding of grief," writes Elizabeth DeVita-

Raeburn in *The Empty Room*, "the important question is not whose loss is the worst but what does this loss, your loss mean to you? The truth is the worst loss is the one that is happening to you, the one that has picked you up and thrown you down and left you struggling to put your life back together."

Finding Albert

Ervin (whose story began this chapter) was filled with hope and dread at the thought of finding his father. When he was in touch with the hope, he had images of the two of them hanging out and doing the sort of things that fathers and sons do together. When in touch with the dread, he fantasized about his father finding out where he lived and coming to take him away and seeking revenge on his mother.

At sixteen, once again our conversations turned to his feelings about his father and his desire to meet him. Finally, Ervin found out through a relative where his father was living. Ervin's father, Albert Munroe, which was Ervin's name before he changed it in his first year of high school, was renting a house owned by one of Ervin's aunts. Ironically, his father's house was right next door to the home where Ervin was born. Ervin decided to write his dad another letter. This one was harder to write, because this time Ervin planned on sending it.

To Albert Munroe,

Hey, Albert. How are you doing? It's me, your son Albert Ervin Munroe. Hi. How has your life been these 16 years? I was just writing to check up on you, see how things were going for you. Me? I'm 16 right now, but I will be 17 on December 5th. If you still remember. From what I hear, I am almost as tall as you are now. I'm 6'2". I sent you a picture along with this letter, so you could get a sense of what

I look like. As you can tell from the picture, I play basket-ball. Lots of it. Last year, as a sophomore on my high school team, I made varsity and got a lot of playing time. I also play the saxophone very well and write music at home using my saxophone a lot. I'm a good student. I get B+'s and A–'s regularly. I am going to be a junior in high school this year. 11th grade. And this is a very big year for me because this is the year that schools look at most when you apply to college. I am going to go to college. Definitely. From what I have heard, you didn't get the chance to go to college but at least now you can say you have a son who is going to college. I know you haven't heard from me in a long time and I know it might be a shock to you. I know it is to me. Just recently I realized that I didn't know any of our family members from your side of the family. So that is why I am writing, to stay in touch with you all down South. That's all. But please do me a big favor, Albert, and write me back. I would really like to hear from you, to know how your life is going. Tell me everything okay?

Sincerely,
Ervin Munroe

Ervin placed the letter inside an envelope along with a recent school picture of himself and one of his CDs, which included a song dedicated to his father. He then wrote the number, city, and zip code of the post office box his mother had rented for him as the return address and handed me the package. "You mail it," he said emphatically.

Any doubts Ervin may have had about his dad's excitement were put to rest when his father's first four letters to Ervin arrived in the same number of days.

His father's response both shocked and surprised Ervin. On the one hand, his father's writing was a kind of stream of con-sciousness. His ideas were rushed and his grammar terrible. Ervin said they reminded him of the kind of correspondence soldiers send their loved ones before going into battle. There were constant references to God, Jesus, hallelujah, peppered with various explanations of how many aunts and uncles Ervin had.

It was tough to decipher the man's scribble. Parts of it felt eerie. Although Ervin had never mentioned his mother in his correspondence, his father expressed his love for her in every letter and how he hoped the three of them could be reunited someday. He referred to himself as "Reverend Albert Munroe" or "Pastor" and addressed Ervin as "Albert" in one sentence and called him "Ervin" in the next.

An honor student educated in private schools, Ervin found his father's poor literary skills alarming. The way the man jumped from topic to topic and his unruly thought process were unnerving enough, but the numerous quotes from the scripture made Ervin especially uncomfortable. Ervin wasn't sure if the letter's chaotic presentation was a result of his father never having received much formal education or a symptom of some sort of thought disorder.

On the other hand, Ervin was deeply touched by his father's enthusiastic response. It had, after all, been almost seventeen years since they had laid eyes on one another.

His father closed all his letters the same way: "I thank the Lord everyday for bringing you back into my life and pray that he arranges for us to meet in person someday soon."

Ervin wrote back that he wanted that too, but needed more time to prepare.

The Visit

Four years passed before Ervin finally arranged to meet his father. At the time, Ervin couldn't say why he waited so long. "It's just not the right time," he replied on the few occasions I asked him. I trust my clients to know when they're ready to take such a big step. If I feel they're avoiding the topic I may bring it up myself, but only so we can discuss their feelings, not to pressure them into making a decision.

However, at the end of his sophomore year of college, Ervin was vacillating more than usual and sought my help. I asked him what he would regret most if he never got to meet his father in person. Ervin, whose talents as a musician had by this time caught up to, if not surpassed, his skills on the basketball court, said that the sound of his father's voice had been an eternal curiosity of his and that he longed to hear it. When I asked Ervin what he feared most about meeting his dad, he said he worried that if he waited too long he might never have the opportunity.

The following week Ervin purchased an airline ticket to Savannah.

Walking up the steps to his father's house, Ervin flashed back on the twenty-one years leading up to this day. The moment he had been waiting his entire life for was just five or six steps away from coming to fruition. Ervin didn't know what to feel or, more important, what he was going say. His tongue felt swollen and numb. His body seemed so heavy, he could barely stand up. The door opened.

"Hi, I'm Erv—"

"Come in, come in," his father interrupted, "I know who you are. Welcome. I've been expecting you." Ervin stepped inside.

Albert Jefferson Munroe, or "AJ," as some of his friends called him, was a very large man. After a life spent playing basketball, Ervin, who was six-foot-four, was accustomed to being the tallest man in a room. His father towered over him. His father's features weren't as soft as Ervin's; still, there was no missing the fact that it was his own face Ervin was staring up at. Ervin remained still for a moment, drinking up the image of his father in front of him, satisfying a thirst he had waited his entire life to quench.

His father seemed to be doing the same, staring in disbelief at the sight of his son standing there in his living room. The man must have weighed close to three hundred pounds, but the way it was spread over his massive frame, he did not look obese. Ervin noticed that his father seemed to be favoring his left leg over his right. The way he had his weight shifted on it gave him an awkward, uncomfortable-looking stance, like the Tin Man in *The Wizard of Oz*.

Everything about his father's body seemed a little dented or busted up, except his eyes. His father's eyes sparkled like those of a kid. In fact, that's exactly what he reminded Ervin of. His father seemed like a big kid trapped in a giant's body. The monster from his youth, whom he had waited his entire life to confront, was a gentle giant.

His father's home looked as if it hadn't been picked up since Ervin had left twenty-one years earlier. Clothes were piled everywhere, and there were musical equipment and amps stacked on every surface of the living room. Come to think of it, it looked just like his own room, thought Ervin, breaking into a smile.

His father had an entire house to himself, but he was only living out of the bedroom. The room was dark, an odd assortment of curtains, sheets, and fabric blocking out any sunlight. All his father's clothes had holes in them. "I'm going to send him a shirt first thing when I get home," thought Ervin.

Opposite the bed was a mantel decorated with every letter and photograph Ervin had ever sent his father. Looking like an art installation, Ervin's CD was displayed prominently in a used deck his father had purchased and placed on a table inside the bay window. It was clearly meant to be the centerpiece of the room.

AJ noticed Ervin staring curiously at the hodgepodge of stereo wires, cables, and electronic equipment. "A guy I know said he can repair that for me so I can listen to it, but for now it gives me pleasure just looking at it," said his father.

Ervin asked his father if he could buy him lunch. His dad did not live in a safe neighborhood, however, and when they walked out of the house the first thing his father did was say hello to the crackhead on the corner, who responded with an enthusiastic: "Hey, AJ!" "How ya doin', brother Nelson," his father said to a man sitting on the sidewalk drinking something out of a brown paper bag. The man answered with a wave and a smile.

His father greeted everyone the same way, brother this and sister that. And everyone said hi back. People seemed to light up at the sound of his father's voice. Suddenly, the whole neighborhood was transformed. They were no longer dangerous people to Ervin, they were just people like him. Instantly, he felt more relaxed, more comfortable in his own skin. For the first time since they'd arrived, Ervin felt that things were going to be okay.

On the way to the restaurant, his father asked if they could make a quick stop. "Do you have time?" his father politely asked. "Here we go. Now it starts. Where is he going to take us?" Ervin thought to himself. They pulled into a 7-Eleven. It took his father five minutes just to get out of the car. They walked into the store. His dad walked like Frankenstein. All of a sudden his father seemed very old to Ervin.

When they finally got inside, the man behind the counter, a man of Pakistani or Indian descent, walked around and greeted Ervin's father and said in a thick accent, "Albert! My good friend Albert!" His father introduced them: "Raj, this is my son Ervin." The man became even more animated. He was hysterical with emotion. He grabbed Ervin's hand and, shaking it vigorously, started repeating the words, "So good to meet you, so good to meet you finally," over and over. And then he said, "Ervin, I have to tell you one thing. This man. Your father, he is a good man. He is my best friend."

That did it. Ervin almost lost it. "My father," he thought, "is somebody's best friend."

"Raj is from India," Ervin's dad pronounced. Ervin wasn't sure, but he thought his father might have winked at him when he said it. "When he came to this country, he didn't have a cent to his name. Now look at him. He owns this place and his brother-in-law runs the Dairy Queen down the block."

Raj showered them with presents. He gave them free sodas and snacks. He opened a disposable camera and took their picture and gave it to them to keep and then handed them another unopened one on their way out the door. "Take pictures, lots of pictures. This is an historic occasion. It is a very special day," he shouted at them as they left the store.

Ervin's father seemed uncomfortable with all of Raj's doting on him and this public display of affection in front of his son. Raj told Ervin that when his store had been the target of a series of small robberies, Albert, a security guard at an area mall, would come to visit him when he got off work. Raj couldn't afford to hire a private security company, and his insurance premiums were being driven through the roof as a result of all the thefts and shoplifting. Albert stayed at the store talking to Raj every night until three or four in the morning, until he was confident that the burglars had moved on to another neighborhood.

Imagining his father, all six-foot-seven of him, standing inside the store in his uniform made Ervin laugh. He must have been a sobering sight to any potential criminals or vandals, he thought to himself.

Ervin wanted to take his father somewhere he would be comfortable, so they went to a fast-food place. Same thing at the restaurant. Everyone knew his father, and his dad knew everyone.

After lunch his father asked him if he wanted to meet some of his relatives. "Sure," replied Ervin, so they drove twenty minutes to a small town called Kingston, where his father's oldest sister, Celina, lived. Ervin's aunt's house was small and run-down. There must have been eleven people living there. If the Board of Health ever showed up, they'd have had a fit, thought Ervin. But it was also a home. The poverty was indeed rough, but it wasn't as depressing or hard to bear as what Ervin had seen up North in the projects, with families all broken apart. He was glad he came from this kind and not the other.

When they opened the screen door at his aunt Celina's house, she was sitting on her sofa watching TV. She didn't notice them come in because people came in and out of her house all day.

"Hi, Celina, I'd like you to meet my son," said AJ. Celina turned slowly so she was facing them, and without skipping a beat said, "He's a fine-looking man, Albert."

At his aunt's and father's urging, Ervin called his cousins, people he'd never met before, and said, "Hi, I'm Albert, I mean AJ Munroe's son, and I'm visiting with him and your mother. . . ." "Oh my God! I'll be right over," was the response he got each time. Gradually the whole house filled up with people.

Sitting in his aunt's house surrounded by all his relatives, Ervin, an only child, remembered thinking how hard it would be to ever feel lonely again.

Ervin promised he would come back the next day and spend some time with his father. After that he would have to go to the airport so he could catch his return flight. But he wasn't sure if he was saying it for his father's benefit or his own. Leaving was going to be harder than he anticipated.

The Journey Home

Alcoholism, drug addiction, mental illness, and childhood abuse can conspire to steal a father's love from a son and render him useless as a parent just as totally and completely as death. Therapy helped Ervin understand that his father was an unfortunate and troubled person who did not have the power to hurt him anymore. If his father had continued to act destructively, Ervin could have walked away from him.

My other client, David, at fifteen, confused and vulnerable and in need of his father's guidance, had his dad torn from the pages of his life in one of the most violent ways imaginable. Gradually, David came to realize that it was not his fault his dad had been so depressed. And more important, that it was his father's responsibility, not David's, to have done something about it.

In the end, neither Ervin nor David remained abandoned, because both men refused to abandon themselves. Each man found ways of rediscovering his father, Ervin through seeking out surrogate dads and, eventually, searching for and finding his own father, and David through his parenting and the myriad ways he continues to show up for his own son.

Standing on the front stoop of his father's house the following morning, Ervin gave his dad a huge bear hug before walking across the lawn to the taxi parked in the driveway.

"Ervin, Ervin, wait!" shouted his father.

"Yeah, Dad?" said Ervin.

"I . . . um . . . I need to tell you something, son," said Albert.

"What is it, Dad?" answered Ervin, thinking it was one last quote of scripture Albert wanted to pass on to his son. He turned toward the house but continued walking backward, because if he didn't leave soon he would miss his flight.

"I wasn't sure if this was the best timing, I was going to wait until later. . . . But if there's a message for me in all this, it's that there is no future, there's only today. . . ." His father's voiced trailed off.

Ervin paused. He walked back toward his father. "I'm listening, Dad, what is it?" he asked, this time with more concern in his voice.

"I'm sick, Ervin. The way I walk, some of it is from playing ball all those years and not taking care of myself, not eating the right things, keeping the weight on . . ."

"Dad, what's wrong? What do you have?"

"Well, I've got cancer, son, it's in my back. But the doctor says that's not where it started. It's in a lot of other places, places you don't want it to be."

"Dad, what does this mean? You're going to be okay, right? I mean they can treat it, can't they?

"The doctor says there's some medicine I have to take at the hospital that can buy me a little time, but he said that there's no recovering from it. Not when it's spread to this much of my body. He said I'm going to die."

"What?!" Ervin felt like he'd been kicked in the stomach.

Albert saw the look on his son's face. And the pain he saw there, he would tell Ervin later, hurt him more than his cancer or anything he had ever experienced, including the day his wife had left him, taking their infant son with her.

"We all have to die, son. I'm not afraid of dying. I look forward to it. I know there's something better waiting for me. I'm just sorry for the timing, that's all. I mean, I had kind of hoped that you and I might have a little more time together. . . ."

"Time? What time? I mean, how much? How much time did the doctor say you have?"

"Three, maybe six—"

"Three years?" Ervin said, cutting his father off. Three, maybe six years? That wasn't as awful as it could be, thought Ervin, although he was starting to feel dizzy.

"Months, son. Three, maybe six months," said his father. "At least, that's what the doctor said. And I have no reason to doubt him. He is a good man. He went to school at UNC and I saw him at a big medical center they have in Atlanta. The doctors in Savannah arranged for me to go there. It took me eight hours by bus."

Ervin cringed at the idea of his father, cancer-ridden, riding the bus alone all the way to Atlanta only to hear this terrible news, and then having to ride the bus by himself all the way home again. He wanted to scream at him, "Why didn't you call me!" But then he realized the absurdity of that idea. He had just met his father for the first time since he was six months old.

When Ervin sat in my office recalling these events, he got as far as the word "cancer" when his voice cracked and his eyes began to tear. My heart sank.

Finding his father was the end of a long journey for Ervin,

and even though they hadn't laid eyes on each other since he was a baby, Ervin couldn't believe how many things they had in common. They had the same eyes, the same smell, and many of the same passions and talents.

Ervin thought about all the opportunities he'd been given to develop his gifts that his father, an impoverished black man living in the South, never had. But nothing was as difficult and painful for Ervin as trying to reconcile the person his father was now with the kind of man he had once been; he was thinking specifically of his father's violent and cruel treatment of his mother.

As troubled as his father had been and, in some instances, still was, it was clear to Ervin that the man his mother had been married to had ceased to exist. The man with whom he had broken bread and whom Ervin had wrapped his arms around would not have done those things to his mother and him when he was a child. And now this.

After resigning himself to spending the rest of his life without hearing the sound of his father's voice or experiencing his father's touch, Ervin had finally found his father. He was somebody's son. It's just that he had counted on being a son for more than a day.

"It's not fair!" protested Ervin. "Why is this happening to me?" he said out loud, his face buried in his hands as he sat on the couch in my office.

Suddenly, it occurred to Ervin that this wasn't happening to him. In fact, it wasn't about him at all. All this time, Ervin thought he had been searching for his father—praying he might find him—so they would have the opportunity to say a simple hello and get to know one another. Now it appeared the opposite was true. He hadn't found his father, his father had found him. After all those years apart, Ervin wasn't calling out to his dad, his dad was calling out to him. And he wasn't calling Ervin to say hello. He was calling him to say good-bye.

Ebbets Field

The most frequent story told about my father's father is the kind of heroic rags-to-riches tale that, if we're to believe what we read in our high school history books, transformed every hard-working immigrant man of his time into a captain of industry, or at least those who wanted success badly enough.

At age fourteen he fled to the United States. An Eastern European Jew from Latvia whose family survived the pogroms of czarist Russia, Walter Diamond arrived in turn-of-the-century New York City with nothing. A scared young man who didn't speak a word of English, he sold newspapers on the streets sixteen hours a day. He married, survived the Depression with a wife and three children, and despite the fact that neither he nor his wife had as much as an eighth grade education, he managed to put all three of his sons through college and graduate school. By the time he died, he was living on Fifth Avenue in a penthouse overlooking Central Park.

They were the American dream.

What my grandfather accomplished was remarkable. But as best I can tell, the only thing more rugged and primitive than the existence he eked out on the streets of New York was the chaotic and unpredictable home life his wife and sons endured while he pulled himself and his family out of poverty.

There were no references to dysfunctional families in my grandfather's time, so I don't know what you would call my father's childhood. My father told me many times that he didn't have the excuse of being the victim of an abusive father to blame his own violent temper on.

These statements were always followed by a story meant to prove his point, but in truth, the stories seemed to contradict him. Such as the time he walked out of a doctor's appointment and found his parents shouting at each other in Yiddish in the waiting room. His mother was standing on a windowsill holding on to the curtains while his father, with one arm wrapped around her legs, hit her repeatedly and tried to pull her down. She was screaming at him to let go of her.

To be fair, not all of Dad's traumas were about family, and many were, in retrospect, quite humorous. One time he was at Ebbets Field watching his beloved Brooklyn Dodgers play the New York Giants. Prior to the game, two sets of men sitting in his section—two white guys rooting for the Dodgers and two black Giants fans—bet on the outcome of the contest.

The one-hundred-dollar bet they laid down was serious money for that time, and the four quickly looked around for a neutral party to hold it for them. One of the Giants' fans said, "How about him," pointing to my father. After they explained that all he had to do to make an easy buck for himself was to be their banker, my father agreed.

Dad sat nervously in his seat the whole game, one hand waving furiously over his head cheering on his team, while his other hand remained shoved deep in his pocket protecting the winners' purse.

Near the end of what was a back-and-forth contest, the Dodgers appeared to put the game away with a three-run homer in the top of the ninth inning. Caught up in the excitement of a Dodgers victory, my father didn't think much of it when the white guy, the Brooklyn fan, said, "That's it, kid, give me my money, I'm going home." At first, my father hesitated, as technically the game wasn't over, but when the man asked him more forcefully, he relented.

What happened next was one of the most remarkable come-from-behind victories in baseball history—the sort of heart-breaking collapse the Dodgers were notorious for. When the game ended with the Giants victorious, the other man and his friend turned to Dad and demanded their winnings. When Dad told them what had happened, they took him back to Harlem as "collateral" and telephoned my grandfather to make good on the bet.

"They were very angry about what happened, but they were never mean to me, all they wanted was their winnings," said Dad. The two men told my grandfather where to bring the money and offered my father something to eat while he waited. My grandfather, who didn't have access to that kind of cash at the time, had to implore a relative to open up his store in order to come up with it all.

Few words were exchanged between father and son when my grandfather arrived with the money. Dad described the hour sub-way ride back to Brooklyn as one of the longest years of his life.

To my grandfather's credit, as Dad was always quick to point out, he didn't call the police. My grandfather was racist to the core, which was just one of the hundreds of things my father and he fought bitterly about. After he brought his son home, he could have gotten his money back and caused the men a great deal of trouble. But my grandfather was also a fair and honest businessman. He saw this as a business deal, pure and simple. The men were only asking for what they had coming to them.

While Dad was, understandably, frightened, even terrified, at moments during the whole ordeal, he always spoke about it with great pride; and he wasn't just being self-aggrandizing. I think he had a special fondness for retelling this story because it was an example of a time when his father was truly there for him. It stood in sharp contrast to my grandfather's violent, crazy behav-ior and Dad's bewildered accounts of it. His father showed up to help his son when he needed him.

4

There's No Place Like Home

LESSONS ON ANGER AND FORGIVENESS

forgiving our fathers

· · · · · · · · · · · · ·

maybe for leaving us too often or
forever when we were little   maybe
for scaring us with unexpected rage
or making us nervous because there seemed
never to be any rage there at all

for marrying or not marrying our mothers
for divorcing or not divorcing our mothers
and shall we forgive them for their excesses
of warmth or coldness   shall we forgive them

for pushing or leaning   for shutting doors
for speaking only through layers of cloth
or never speaking or never being silent

in our age or theirs or in their deaths
saying it to them or not saying it
if we forgive our fathers what is left?

—DICK LOURIE

ANGER, AT LEAST AS IT'S traditionally thought of in the context of death and dying, refers to the phase of mourning when, after denying it, we finally inherit the massive loss confronting us. It's the moment when each one of us is given permission to act out our own personal Greek tragedy of pain and suffering, to look up at the stars and the heavens and call out in anger, "Why me!?"

Unfortunately, for men, rarely is anger a stepping stone from one affective state to another. Instead, it's the manifestation of every feeling they experience, because for many men the only acceptable emotion to show is anger. It reminds me of a greeting card I used to have on my refrigerator. On the cover are a dozen identical drawings of the same Irish setter, its tongue hanging out and an adoring but clueless expression on its face. Underneath each frame is the name of an emotion: joy, sadness, love, hate, anger, depression, rage, happiness, confusion, and so on. The caption reads: "The moods of an Irish setter."

No emotion blocks men's grief more than anger, and none is more elusive than forgiveness. Men often use anger in a type of "one size fits all" fashion, choosing to express their emotions this way regardless of what they're feeling. James Baldwin wrote, "I imagine one reason people cling to their hates so stubbornly is because they sense, once the hate is gone, they will be forced to deal with the pain." Many adult sons discover that coming to terms with the anger they feel toward their fathers is like peeling the layers of an onion; underneath the skin exist other feelings no less compelling, each one closer to the core.

For men who grew up knowing too much of our fathers' anger, we're afraid of becoming like our dads. It's an understandable fear. But we create what we defend against, so it should come as no surprise when we become those angry men.

The Father Dance

Throughout my career, colleagues have been quick to comment on my ability to remain calm in the face of a crisis. For many therapists, working with angry and violent men or families who are trying to mend from years of alcoholism and abuse is like falling out of the sky and finding themselves in a foreign land where everything seems strange, frightening, and unpredictable. "How," they ask, "are you able to keep your wits about you? How do you manage to stay so composed when you're sitting with such violent and chaotic families in which people are actively yelling, belittling, and threatening to physically attack one another?

"There's no place like home," I reply.

In *I Don't Want to Talk about It: Overcoming the Secret Legacy of Male Depression*, therapist and author Terry Real speaks eloquently about the dance of violence and intimacy that men who grew up in abusive homes grapple with:

> Too often what fathers bequeath to their children is their own unacknowledged pain, and in instances of violence, an entitlement to inflict it on others. The frightening reality that must be faced is that when a boy is emotionally or physically abused by his father, one avenue for obtaining closeness with him, for absolving the father, and uniting with him is to become him.

In my dad's case, sometimes I could actually see this struggle taking place inside him; watch him trying not to overreact or erupt in an outburst of verbal or physical abuse. It was those moments, when reason won out, that I appreciated him most.

Like Real, I figured out very early on that I could try to help men like my father or I could become my father. This seed was first planted in my head by a social worker Dad and I went to see following my parents' divorce.

Shirley Stein was a friend of my mother's and a child therapist with an excellent reputation. When my mother first sent me to Shirley, I was desperate for reassurance from someone that I was going to turn out all right. As a result of my parents' divorce, everywhere I went I felt as if I wore a scarlet "D" around my neck. All I wanted was to feel "normal," which to a thirteen-year-old means to fit in and not draw attention to oneself. Unfortunately, at the time, my only idea of what therapy was about came from the group therapy sessions I watched on *The Bob Newhart Show*, which scared the bejesus out of me, as the oddball cast of characters assembled there seemed everything but normal.

When I arrived for my first appointment, Shirley hobbled out of her office, her legs harnessed into a pair of metal braces and her arms precariously balanced on a pair of matching steel crutches. When she held out her hand to greet me, I had two thoughts. The first was to turn and flee. The second was that this was clearly a woman who knew something about what it felt like to feel different. By the end of our session, her braces looked like angels' wings to me, signifying safety and comfort.

Shirley was one of the first therapists I encountered as an adult or child who had no need to pretend she was the magnificent Oz—pulling levers behind a curtain, providing everyone with solutions to whatever ailed them. Instead, she viewed therapy as a collaborative effort, trusting that the answers to my questions resided inside me and that all I needed was the opportunity to discover them.

For our last visit, Shirley suggested my father join us. During the meeting Dad sat dutifully while I expressed my anger at him for how he treated our mother and the way he raged at us all the time. I cried my way through most of the session. Mostly, what I remember is my father holding me while I sobbed and sobbed until it was time to go.

You Can Go Home Again

Almost twenty years later, the week before I was to be married, Dad asked me to return to see Shirley with him. For years I'd been expecting this. I just wasn't expecting it the week of my wedding. I remember thinking that this had to be the worst possible timing. But my father had never asked me to go to therapy. After years of waiting for him to do so, Dad was finally taking the initiative toward our doing something to mend our past, and I didn't want to pass up the opportunity.

This time, Shirley wheeled her way to the front door to greet us. She acknowledged the look on my face before I had a chance to say anything. "You haven't seen me since I've become wheelchair bound have you?" she said. "I'm sorry, I just wasn't expecting it," I answered embarrassedly.

"Well, I don't think it would make any difference in our case, Jonathan, as chair or no chair, it's pretty clear I'd be looking up at you. You've gone through a few changes yourself since I saw you last, wouldn't you say?" she said, holding out her arms to offer me a hug. I bent over and gave her an awkward embrace. Sliding my hand between her and the back of her chair felt too intimate, so I wrapped my arms around the entire wheelchair with her in it as if I were preparing to pick up an oversized piece of living room furniture.

As it turned out, it wasn't the past Dad wanted to talk about. It was something about our relationship in the present that was upsetting him. I'm embarrassed to say I no longer remember what it was. It might have been about the wedding. I remember him feeling that we were only interested in hearing about the financial contribution he intended to make but not his opinions about anything else.

Whatever it was, I remember feeling relieved. I was imagining something horrific. Some earth-shattering revelation about my true nature that he needed to warn me about. And then I remember thinking that it didn't matter what it was.

There was something that felt right about the two of us sitting in Shirley's office on the eve of this important rite of passage in my life (and his). Last time we were unpacking a divorce, this time it was a wedding. His son was getting married. I was the same age my father had been when my mother and he exchanged vows. There we were, just the two of us, with all our hopes, dreams, and fears—past, present, and future.

Once again, I found myself crying with my father in Shirley's office. And just as before, my father held me.

Through my tears, I managed to tell him that I was terrified of becoming like him. His violence hovered like a dark cloud over my life, casting its shadow over all my intimate relationships. I told him I was scared. I worried there was some kind of . . . I don't know what . . . some kind of recessive gene or something in the back of my brain that was going to be released when I got married and cause me to behave like him; something that was going to transform me into something monstrous.

I don't recall much else we talked about. But I remember the words Shirley spoke when I was finished. She looked me in the eyes and said, "Jonathan, I understand why you would be afraid of that happening, anyone would under the circumstances. But it's not going to happen. You and your Dad are two very different people. You carry the same wounds from childhood, you both came from emotionally and physically abusive families, but for some reason—and don't ask me to explain why—you've done very different things with those experiences. You are not the same kind of man as your father in that regard. There may be things you admire about him, other ways in which you're alike, but that's not one of them."

Salvation.

The Sunflower

Not every man's anger, or even his rage, toward his father is the result of his father's abusive or shameful treatment of him.

Sam, a small roundish man, had a youthful face with a wise look about it. He was a little disheveled in his appearance, but his unkempt hair and unfashionable dress could not hide his handsome features. He reminded me of a good-looking rabbinical scholar. He reminded me of my father. As Sam entered my office, I noticed he was holding a book in his hands. I recognized its bright yellow jacket and black lettering right away as Simon Wiesenthal's *The Sunflower: On the Possibilities and Limits of Forgiveness*.

I was very familiar with this book. It is about the author's experience of being imprisoned in a Nazi concentration camp. The book takes its title from the following scene. En route from the camp to the grounds of a hospital the prisoners were maintaining, Wiesenthal passed a military cemetery. On each grave there was planted a sunflower.

Suddenly, he found himself envying the dead soldiers, who each had a sunflower to connect him to the living world and butterflies to visit his grave. "For me there would be no sunflower. I would be buried in a mass grave, where corpses would be piled on top of me. No sunflower would ever bring light into my darkness, and no butterflies would dance on my dreadful tomb."

One day he was taken from his work detail to the bedside of a dying member of Hitler's notorious SS. Haunted by the crimes in which he had participated, the soldier wanted to confess and obtain absolution from a Jew. Wiesenthal said nothing. But even years after the war had ended, he wondered: Had he done the right thing?

He poses the same question to his readers, asking us what we would have done in his place. In his book, fifty-three distinguished men and women respond to his questions. They include theologians, political leaders, writers, jurists, psychiatrists, human rights activists, Holocaust survivors, and victims of attempted genocide in Bosnia, Cambodia, China, and Tibet.

I had barely sat down when Sam said, "Can you help me learn how to forgive?" The way he phrased the words, it felt more like a challenge than a question. He was sitting on the edge of the couch as he spoke them. He took his time, rolling his tongue around each one like he had a mouth full of hard candies, before delivering them one at time, sounding out every vowel and consonant.

When finished, he sank back into my sofa, legs crossed and arms folded, looking satisfied that he had done what he had come to do. It seemed as if he thought his job was over now and that I should know what to do or say next.

"If you want to work on forgiveness," I said, eyeing the book resting in his lap, "you might want to start with someone or something a little less troublesome than the Nazis. Like maybe the postman who is supposed to show up at ten-thirty every morning but never makes it to your house before noon?" Sam laughed and said, "It is not the Nazis I need to forgive, it's my father."

Sam's father had died ten years earlier from cancer. Sam said he was embarrassed that after all this time, his father's death continued to be the source of so much anguish for him.

I was angry with him for nine years. I was angry because he concealed his knowledge of his worsening condition without trying to seek treatment. How could he do this to me? How could he abandon me so suddenly? Why didn't he give me a chance to say goodbye? He knew that he was dying. Didn't he have some sense that how he dies would have meaning for me?

The writer Anne Lamott said forgiveness is giving up all hope of having had a better past. It also means letting go of the possibility of changing it. In Sam's case, we might say that forgiveness was giving up all hope of his father having had a better death. Sam and I agreed he couldn't change the past but he could change how he felt about it, and that's what we set out to do in our sessions together.

In a process I would describe as a slow, gradual, elusive *becoming*, Sam began making peace with his father's death.

> When my father died, the whole deck got reshuffled. Everything about my father I thought was a certain way changed in one moment. Gradually, I'm starting to realize that I don't have to be so mad at him anymore; for leaving me the way he did or for being who he was. It's not like I forgot all my disappointment. But that disappointment is less important than how he cherished me, and I cherished him.

Three months after our therapy ended, Sam sent me a card letting me know he had done something he had never been able to do before: he went to visit the cemetery where his father was buried. Like the sunflowers planted on the graves of the German soldiers in Wiesenthal's story, nine years after his father's death, Sam planted his feet firmly atop his father's grave and grieved his dreadful loss.

"The capacity to love over time entails the capacity to tolerate and repair hatred," wrote the analyst Stephen Mitchell. He was writing about romantic relationships, but his words apply to any intimate relationships that are important to us, no matter what challenges they present. The force with which these kinds of feelings manifest in a relationship will determine the nature of the repairing that needs to be undertaken, but it is not something that only affects relations where abuse has occurred. Being able to experience love and hatred both at the same time, and toward the same person, is part of what it means to be human. The presence of real violence in father-son relations complicates this picture and our capacity to maintain and repair hatred, but it does not diminish our need to do so.

Soul Repairs

The first thing you notice about Patrick when he enters a room is his size. Physically, he is a very imposing man. The second is the size of his spirit. It lights up the room. A gentle, peace-loving person, he is a gifted therapist and healer who has devoted his life to helping others.

Although Patrick's dad was a working-class Irishman who worked on the docks (a longshoreman) and mine a Jewish university professor, we discovered that our fathers were more alike than different. Born and raised in Brooklyn, they had similar temperaments. While Patrick's dad was a hard-drinking man—"a tough guy," as Patrick put it—and more prone to physical violence than my father, we both agreed the angry words and constant verbal abuse were more damaging than either man's touch.

Patrick spent the better part of his adult life trying to repair his relationship with his father. This pursuit took on a sense of urgency for Patrick when his father was diagnosed with end-stage cancer. Eventually, he came to view his attempts to make peace with his father's memory as a spiritual quest of sorts, one he considered abandoning on numerous occasions. And given his father's past behavior, had he done so, no one would have thought the worse of him.

In the course of our conversation, Patrick talked about the pain he experienced when an affair he was having broke up his first marriage. Patrick described these events and the turmoil they caused his family as the most difficult period of his life.

Patrick's two sons, just twelve and sixteen years old at the time, were furious with him and, said Patrick, "understandably sided with their mother." For months neither boy would speak to him. Patrick didn't understand how this could be happening. He was a therapist, someone who helped people mend, not someone who hurt them. When he realized that something he had done, that his choice to end his marriage and leave his wife for someone else—a woman he eventually married—was the cause of so much suffering and upheaval in his sons' lives, he was devastated. The shame was so unbearable, he became suicidal.

Ironically, Patrick identifies that moment as the turning point in his relationship with his father. Up to that time he had had a very one-dimensional view of his father. Patrick described an invisible plumb line that ran down the middle of their relationship, dividing all their interactions into "good" and "evil," with his father representing the devil and Patrick the angel.

Growing up with an abusive father, Patrick had sworn this would never happen to him. As an adult, every significant action he took in his life had to pass a litmus test demonstrating that it was the exact opposite of how his father would have behaved if presented with the same circumstances. And while it was true that, like his dad, he had developed a serious drinking problem, at least he wasn't an angry drunk the way his father had been.

All this changed for Patrick when he discovered he had hurt his sons in such a profound fashion. "I couldn't have betrayed my children that way," he told himself. "That's the kind of father my old man was, not me." All of a sudden, for the first time in his life, he found himself strongly identifying with his father. And while it was important to recognize their differences—for example, Patrick never resorted to physical violence—this fact brought him little comfort.

As a result of his affair, Patrick had become to his own sons what his father had always represented for him: he was the man responsible for his sons' most traumatic memory.

Patrick's story had a profound effect on me. It started me thinking about the moments in my life that resulted in my experiencing intense shame because of something I did to someone else; some interaction with a loved one in which I betrayed their trust or transgressed their boundaries in a way that hurt or injured them.

While I found this an exquisitely painful task, it was not a difficult one. There were many to choose from. But now, instead of using my father's failures and shortcomings to erect walls between us, I look for ways they connect us. And as with Patrick, this process of reconciliation did not end when my father died. If anything, it has become a more prevalent theme since his death.

For years I felt intense shame as a result of my father's violence and the traumas I experienced at his hand. Alice Walker says that shame is the result of soul injury. Healing from shame and trauma requires soul repair. And that is what I'm attempting to do here. I'm trying to write my father's violence out of my life, or at least the effects of that violence. And I'm endeavoring to do so by leaning into the experience, not running from it.

Most of the men whose stories are collected in this book managed to repair their connection to their fathers and/or themselves in ways that added beauty to the relationship. Each son reached beyond his own and his father's tale of suffering and grief and found something meaningful to take away from it.

When mourning, we honor the parts of ourselves that seem irreparable. We don't apologize for them or try to disguise them in an effort to mend them in some seamless way. "There is a crack in everything. It's how the light gets in," said Leonard Cohen.

Mourning brings light into our darkness.

—————

The Piano Lesson

It was a cold February morning when my dad received word his father was dead. He had been killed running to catch a bus. My grandfather wasn't fleeing muggers or rushing to the hospital to donate a kidney to a dying patient, he was going to his office in downtown Manhattan as he had every day for the past fifty years. He had just finished walking the forty blocks he always traveled by foot (to save money) and arrived at his bus stop just as a bus was pulling away. He was running alongside it, banging on the doors and shouting obscenities at the driver, when the vehicle turned, knocking him to the ground. He died the instant his head hit the curb. The driver never saw him. He was eighty-three years old.

Three years prior, Dad had started making weekly trips into the city to visit his father. Knowing there was little love lost between the two, I asked Dad why he had bothered. He said he felt bad for my grandfather, a widower, who, ever since my grandmother had died, spent most of his days alone. He also wanted to get to know the man better. He knew it wasn't going to be easy, but he wanted to try.

These were not great meetings of the mind. My grandfather did not share my father's enthusiasm for philosophy, great litera-ture, or sports. He wasn't interested in politics and didn't under-stand his son's commitment to social justice or any of the other causes Dad championed. In fact, the two had almost nothing in common, except music; they were both passionate about it.

Unfortunately, with the exception of Dad's disastrous encounter with a violin in his youth, neither man could hold a tune or play a note. Until my grandfather got the idea that he wanted to take up piano. He was in his seventies. He took lessons and worked hard at it. One day I accompanied Dad on his weekly visit to hear him play.

For someone who hadn't been playing very long, my grandfather had quite the venue for his recital. The floor-to-ceiling windows in the living room of my grandparents' penthouse opened to a terrace with a view of the reservoir in Central Park and the city's skyline. After my father and I were seated, my grandfather took his place at a baby grand Steinway positioned prominently in the center of the room. My grandfather's eyes danced and glistened as he banged his stiff, swollen fingers up and down the ebony and ivory keys.

Five minutes of listening to my grandfather's playing was all I needed to appreciate what a labor of love this was on my father's part. But one look was all it took to see what it meant to my grandfather that his son wanted to spend time with him this way.

5

How Deep Is the Well?

HEALING LONELINESS, EMPTINESS, AND DESPAIR

I have woven a parachute out of everything broken.

—WILLIAM STAFFORD

"WHEN WILL I START to feel better?" is the question I most frequently encounter in my practice in general and in my work with grieving sons in particular. The answer is a tough one.

Arthur Koestler, in an essay in which he wondered whether humankind would go the way of the dinosaur, formulated what he called the dinosaur's prayer: "Lord, a little more time!" Men don't need words and images to work out their grief. They need time. The time needed to slowly, gradually, painstakingly unravel feelings knotted in what seems like a hopeless tangle. Feelings of betrayal, frustration, hurt, rage, agony, and joy. These moments in therapy when a person feels truly alone with his grief remind me of the author Audre Lorde's words: "For the embattled there is no place that cannot be home nor is."

Since my father's death, I divide the events in my life into two categories—the ones that happened before he died and those that happened after. Initially, there was relief. No more unexpected trips to New Jersey or Solomon-like decisions where I had to choose between lying next to my newborn's crib and lying next to my father's hospital bed. But without these dilemmas to occupy my thoughts, I didn't know what to do with myself. I was lost. For the longest time, I gave up all hope of ever getting my life back. It didn't seem possible. No matter how much I "returned to normal," the one person I felt I needed was not going to return.

The first time I got a sense that my old self might still be out there somewhere waiting for me to reclaim it was simply a glimpse. I was talking with (read "at") my own therapist. It had been a very stressful week in my practice. All my clients seemed to be in crisis at once, my writing wasn't going well, and I was complaining about a colossal money problem (I can't remember what it was now).

All of a sudden, in the middle of all my whining, this very familiar feeling came over me—like a wave at the beach that knocks you down and then leaves all this seaweed and sand in your suit and hair to remember it by. I stopped talking and realized it had been more than a year since I'd gotten this worked up about what one author of those pithy inspirational pocket books calls "the small stuff." It wasn't an epiphany, but it was my life and I'd missed it. My father was still dead and all the stupid details that make up our world were starting to matter to me again. Words can't describe how relieved I was to discover this.

The death of a loved one is a crash course in Buddhism. It brings into focus what things are important and really matter to you. Seeing life with this kind of sharpness and clarity all the time is exhausting. We need the contrast. Sure, I have an earnest desire to save the world, but there are times when the most reality I can handle is finding out which contestant is going to make it to the next round of *American Idol*. So while I was grateful for the lessons and wisdom my father's death provided me, it was a relief to see that I was still capable of sweating the small stuff.

How do we arrive at this place in our healing? How do we move from the discovery of yet another regret, precious possession, or heart-wrenching memory we won't be able to share with our fathers to restoring some semblance of sanity, if not serenity, to our everyday lives? This chapter provides some answers—but first, another story.

Lyra and Vega

From the time my son Julian was seven months old, he had a babysitter who, with the exception of my best friend Prudence, was the only person we ever left him with. In my first book I referred to Lyra as the "childcare goddess" because that's what she was. When Julian was two and my wife was pregnant again, we looked forward to our new baby—a boy we named Oliver— enjoying the same kind of relationship with her. But then something wonderful and something terrible occurred which prevented that from happening: Lyra became pregnant herself, and a short time after, her father was diagnosed with terminal cancer.

Lyra's father, Clark Johnson, was an editor and journalist at our local paper who was admired and loved by many. He was also an excellent amateur astronomer. During this stressful period, Lyra had a baby girl. She named her Vega after one of the stars in the constellation Lyra, which is how Clark had found her name. Vega's first two years were her grandfather's last. He died three months shy of his granddaughter's second birthday.

I've always enjoyed a close connection with Vega. She is a wonderful child. When she was younger, she was just like my son Julian and, if you believe what Vega's grandmother says, just like Lyra. Vega was what we might call a little "high maintenance." So during Clark's memorial service, when Vega was giving her handlers a hard time, I took her to a childproof room in the back of the church where all the toys belonging to the day care center were set up. She and I had a grand time. We even got to watch some of the ceremony together, standing in the doorway that separated the child care area from the chapel. When the minister asked if anyone had any personal stories they wanted to share about Clark, this is the story I told.

At the time my younger son, Oliver, was eight months and Julian was two, I was shopping around my proposal for this book. After many rejections and a few near misses, I finally found someone I thought would be the right person to represent the project. Better yet, she lived nearby so I could meet with her in person. We scheduled lunch at a deli in a town close to both of us. I arranged for a sitter to watch Julian and decided to bring Oliver with me to the meeting because he was a *good* baby, which in parent-speak means "compliant," and what is more important, a good napper.

Fifty minutes before I was supposed to be at the meeting, my sitter canceled. She had a good excuse, but I was too busy picturing her starring in one of those horror films with names like *No One Can Hear You Scream* or *Dawn of the Dead* to listen to what it was. "Okay, Jon, no need to panic," I said to myself, "you can call Lyra. When I explain my situation, she will understand; and better yet, she'll be able to watch both kids!" It was a fail-safe plan with only one problem: Lyra wasn't home. Normally that would deter me, but not this time. I called everywhere and everyone. I thought of calling the state police. I finally reached Clark, who offered Lyra's younger brother's services.

It was back to plan A. Oliver would come with me to the meeting and Julian could stay with Lyra's kid brother Dillon, whom Julian called "Dee Dee" and totally adored. The problem was, Clark didn't know where Dillon was either. I resisted the urge to report him to social services or ask him what kind of a father lets his thirteen-year-old son bicycle unsupervised in a bucolic rural New England village on a warm, lazy day in summer.

Three phone calls later with no sign of Dillon or Lyra, I found myself asking Clark in a voice that may have sounded a little like begging if there was any way he might consider watching Julian for me. I shared my whole saga, hoping there might be some kind of oath reporters take in journalism school to help out their fellow writers.

Clark didn't skip a beat. "Well, it's been a while since I've had a two-year-old, Jonathan, but sure, why not, bring him over." Ecstatic, I went out to start my car and—I feel like Dave Barry as I find myself wanting to write "*I'm not making this up*"—the car wouldn't start.

I called my neighbors, who are angels who have to live here with us on Earth because they ran out of room in heaven, and in moments I had a car. And not just any car. I had their aging mother's yellow, mint-condition Cadillac Seville. It was the kind of automobile Southern ladies drive to church on Sundays. My wife said it looked like a giant Easter egg with caramel filling, referring to the beige leather seats. I piled the kids inside and headed over to Clark's house.

En route, I explained to Julian that I couldn't find Lyra, but he was going to get to play with Lyra's daddy for a few hours. "You'll have fun, honey," I said, trying to comfort him. He wasn't buying it, and started to protest. "This is a *really* important meeting, sweetie, please do this just this one time for Daddy," I pleaded.

By the time we got to Clark's, Julian seemed resigned if not happy about the idea. What's more, he and Clark had a blast until about halfway through the visit when, according to Clark, Julian said he'd had fun but he was going home now and proceeded to start walking down the driveway. When Clark told him he had to wait for me to return, Julian burst into tears.

When I picked up Julian, I was overwhelmed with gratitude. I couldn't thank Clark enough. And I didn't think there was any way I could ever repay him—until I found myself standing in the church holding his two-year-old granddaughter in my arms telling this story.

My reason for sharing it now is to underscore that it's never too late to have an important conversation with someone after they die, resolve a conflict, pay back a debt, return a favor, make amends, forgive them, share a joke, or simply tell them you love them. The notion that we have only a finite amount of time to make our peace with our fathers before they die, or to honor their memories after they're gone, and the kind of pressure this type of thinking puts on us when we're trying to grieve, is not only unnecessary, it's simply not true.

Healing Stories, Not Cliffs Notes

"So long as there is a sheet of paper and a pen, there is always a way out." This is counsel I find myself repeating over and over in my practice. I encourage people to use letter writing for all sorts of problems they face in their lives, from addiction and depression to trauma and grief. Letter writing is something I often find myself reaching for when trying to help teenage boys and adult men honor their relationships with their fathers, both living and dead.

This includes the intense anguish we experience following the sudden death of a loved one or the anticipatory grief we suffer when caring for an ill or dying parent. Because each person will bring different hopes, anxieties, and histories to his or her letter, there is no blueprint for using this approach productively.

Letters are healing stories, not Cliffs Notes. If they collapse time and allow a son to heal his relationship with his estranged father (living or dead) more quickly, that's terrific, but that is not my intention. Like mourning, therapy ought to be a time-sensitive, not a time-driven, process.

In the current age of managed health care we work and live in, I often find myself explaining to participants at my workshops that I don't have billable hours in my practice, I have billable moments. And the writing gifted me by my clients and presented here represent some of my best ones. After circulating these doc-uments to a larger audience, I'm frequently asked what I actually do with someone's letter once they've finished reading it to me.

Typically, the questioner is not asking how you perform ther-apy with a man grieving the loss of his father or with a client try-ing to let go of his or her addiction. Most therapists know how to assist a bereaved child or adult son who has lost his father, and they make very capable allies regardless of the problems their clients face. What people usually mean when they ask me this is: What do you do in those moments, Jonathan, when after reveal-ing something in a letter, an individual comes unraveled in your office because he or she has never shared feelings that painful with another living soul before?

Most of the problems we experience in life are the result of our running from or trying to avoid pain. So just staying with whatever feelings surface on the page, and remaining present for our clients while they attempt to do the same, is a very powerful intervention in and of itself, and is often enough. We're not required to take any action. All we need to do is witness and pro-vide the binding of a safe, caring, and knowledgeable relationship to hold the pages of their stories together.

"Good-bye Dad, I Love You"

When I first began working with seventeen-year-old Randy, a wary, uncommunicative high-school athlete, he was smoking pot daily and using cocaine on weekends. He hung out with a rough crowd and had serious problems at home, including a moody, vio-lent stepfather and a mother who dealt drugs to pay the rent. In Randy's mind, I was just another adult he was forced to tolerate. His only motivation for joining my group for substance-abusing kids—the result of a school referral—was to keep from being kicked off the football team.

Several weeks into the group, Randy revealed that three years earlier, his father had died of AIDS from IV drug use. His public attitude about his dad's untimely death was stoic: "Shit happens." But he also told the group that when his father was alive, the two had spent little time together. In fact, one of the only things Randy knew about his dad was that he did drugs. It occurred to me that at an unconscious level, perhaps Randy's own drug use was a kind of desperate bid to maintain some connection to his lost father. If so, I thought it might help him to try to contact his father at a deeper level. For many people, drugs serve as stand-ins for human relationships they haven't yet dared to create. But for other people, substances provide a kind of distorted connection with a critically important person who is already in their lives.

On a hunch, I asked Randy to write a letter to his dad. "What kind of relationship would you have liked to have had with him?" I gently asked. "Write to him about that." After some initial eye rolling and foot-dragging, Randy brought in his letter:

Dear Dad,

I wish you would have came to me instead of just running away from me. I would have loved to been with you. I just wanted to be your son. When I spent time with you it was great. And now you are gone and I will never see you again: I wish you were here now because I could realy use you as my dad. Even though you whernt around when I was younger I could use you. You could make up for it now I miss you so much.

Randy

When I asked Randy to read the letter aloud in group, he got as far as the second sentence when his voice broke and his eyes filled up with tears. The group of kids was silent, utterly present with him as he half-read, half-wept his letter. As I sat with them in the circle, absorbing Randy's torrent of grief and loss, I was reminded why I so persistently encourage clients in my groups to read their letters out loud. Again and again, I find that when feelings move from the heart to paper, then from paper to spoken word, our felt connection with our experience deepens. And when other people witness that experience, our capacity to embrace our own pain—and the caring of others—deepens still more. Bearing witness is a very profound thing to do for another human being, and we don't forget the people who have done this for us.

Randy didn't forget. After that session, he slowly began to let go of some of his bravado and stoicism. He brought the letter to our next several group meetings and started sharing more about his dad. He began, also, to soften noticeably toward me. Where in the past, I had been a tolerable but essentially clueless adult, now, as a result of several conversations we had about his letter, Randy began to trust me with parts of himself he had carefully edited out before.

For me, the turning point in our new, trusting relationship was the day Randy invited me to come to one of his football games. I wasn't his dad, but at that moment, I was a good enough stand-in. I went to the game and cheered like a madman.

This slow tending and deepening of my relationship with Randy, culminating in the re-parenting he allowed me to do, embodies for me both the limits and the power of letter writing to create change. If I had merely instructed Randy to write a letter to his dad with minimal follow-up, I would have continued to be a meaningless, expendable adult in his life. But when I asked him to read it aloud, the letter became vital in our work together because it allowed Randy to uncover and experience his longing for his dad, which in turn created a space for a relationship with an adult man who was willing to care for and guide him. His letter wasn't therapy, but it created a generous, fruitful opening for therapy.

Another seventeen-year-old client, Craig, whose father died of cirrhosis, wrote the following letter:

Dear Dad,
There are a few things I wish you had considered while you were alive. I wish you would have realized that you were an alcoholic. You should have been responsible about your health and you would have still been here today. If you had just remembered my birthday or Christmas once, I would have been so happy. Although I wasn't the greatest of kids, I was there when you needed me, and always loved you more than any person on the face of the earth. But I do thank you for everything you did do.

Love you Dad,
Craig

For Craig and Randy, in the absence of more permanent structures in their lives, the letters provided a kind of makeshift memorial honoring the powerful presence of each child's connection to his deceased father. Craig attended the same group as Randy. A question both boys were asked frequently in and outside of group was, if given the chance to do things over, would they want different fathers? Not surprisingly, neither boy knew what to say. It felt like an impossible choice. Implicit in such queries is another question: Why grieve such disappointing men? While I couldn't answer for them, I imagined that more than wanting different fathers, what each young man truly desired was for his father to be different.

The assumption that the people who ask me the "trading places" question always make is that I would have gotten something or somebody better. Of course, we have no way of knowing that. I know I could have done a lot worse.

A father who physically or emotionally abuses his son does

untold damage to his child's healthy sense of self, including his ability to trust, his belief in his personal safety, and his experience of the world as a meaningful place. Mourning an abusive father is an attempt to take back as much as possible of what was robbed. However, it does not mean we wish to have the same father back (or one who behaves the same way).

Writing their stories down in the form of a letter can help sons like Randy and Craig (and Ervin)—recovering from legacies of abuse, addiction, and abandonment—put words to previously indescribably terrible events and feelings, what the analyst Melanie Klein called our "unthinkable agonies." No activity is more essential to a person's recovery from pain and trauma than the act of naming and putting words to one's traumatic experience. When wrapped in a narrative and fashioned into a story, the trauma loses its grip on the person's past and gives new meaning to his life.

The Storytelling Circle

Sharing our feelings with people who can relate based on their own similar experiences can be extremely valuable when grieving. This explains why women with breast cancer are so helped by Reach to Recovery groups, and why the group experience is the foundation of Alcoholics Anonymous recovery programs.

Another activity that can help decrease the sense of loneliness and isolation a man feels after his father dies is the storytelling circle. After his father died, one client of mine organized this kind of gathering for his immediate family and invited his other relatives as well as his father's coworkers to participate.

After everyone had arrived, James lit a candle in the middle of a circle while one of his father's brothers offered a blessing.

James asked each participant to think about a question ahead of time that he or she wanted to put to the group.

For example, tell us about the most extraordinary day you spent with our father, or tell us about the bravest or most loving thing you ever saw our father do. "At first there was silence, but once the stories began we got lost in them," recalled James. Later he collected them in writing and put them together in a "Book of Remembrance."

James asked his young nieces and nephews to help decorate and design the book. One of his sisters organized a separate circle for the children and helped them write their stories down and draw pictures to go with them. When they were finished, they also put them in the book. James's mother added treasured letters and photographs from a life spent with her husband.

Rituals like these provide us with ways of connecting with other people. Most men I see are terribly alone in their grief. They're like castaways, each one occupying his own tiny island of heartache and sadness.

Rituals help link our experience to other men's stories, transforming our disparate isles of sorrow into archipelagos of mourning. Churches, synagogues, and sanghas can provide safe spaces for performing such ceremonies. For many, religion offers the sort of witnessing and holding I'm thinking of through the practice of its daily rituals and traditions. However, anything can be a ritual if family members put energy into making it meaningful.

After Nick's father died (Nick and Crash were the father and son duo whose stories were introduced in chapter 2), Nick described an evening spent with his brothers and sisters getting drunk together around a fire on the beach (Nick drank seltzer), smoking cigarettes and remembering their father. This is a ritual too, and no less sacrosanct. Nick treasured the time with his brothers and sisters and the stories they shared about their dad. Stories stay with us. Many years later, Nick and his siblings still have theirs and always will.

Heart Advice for Difficult Times

Several years ago, my friend Andrea's brother died. James (Hap) Hairston was a veteran of New York's tabloid wars who oversaw numerous Pulitzer Prize–winning stories at *Newsday* and later at its across-town rival the *Daily News*. He worked tirelessly to improve every story one line at a time. Until a heart attack slowed him, this jazz-loving editor lapped up life as a big-city newspaperman. He played himself as an extra in the 1994 movie *The Paper*, starring Michael Keaton, and he starred in a clothing ad for big men. "They used people who were big in size and also big in life," said his wife. Hap's reporters either loved and respected him or hated and respected him. But this wisecracking taskmaster had a softer side many never saw until his father died.

After his father passed away, Hap began caring for his ailing mother. He wrote a piece to help her cope with her loss. Later he used it as the basis for a larger story on the tragedy at the World Trade Center, which plunged Hap—still reeling from the death of his father just days before—and his beloved city into a state of grief and despair. He died a year later.

"This will not be easy," he wrote. "Once you begin to grieve a certain tragedy, you risk opening the floodgates to unfelt, unexpressed and unhealed inner angst from the other traumatic events in your life." Hap was a man whose words inspired others to do their best work. Andrea shared these particular lines at their mother's memorial service. Hearing them read out loud, I realized Hap's story, written for his fellow New Yorkers after 9/11, was also a powerful meditation on the death of his father that we can use to help guide us through our process:

> That we can grieve and recover often seems an amazing feat, yet human resilience is amazing. Just as a forest can burn to the ground and eventually grow anew, or a town can be devastated by a flood and rebuild, so each of us can

be overcome by our grief, have the enormity of our loss overwhelm us, and eventually recover and restore our lives. This is nature's way.

Grief is a wound that needs attention in order to heal. To work through and complete grief means to face our feelings openly and honestly, to express or release our feelings fully, and to tolerate and accept our feelings for however long it takes for the wound to heal. For most of us, that is a big order. Therefore, it takes courage to grieve. It takes courage to feel our pain and to face the unfamiliar. It also takes courage to grieve in a society that mistakenly values restraint, where we risk the rejection of others by being open and different. Open mourners are a select group, willing to journey into pain and sorrow in order to recover.

Unfortunately, our misconceptions about grief keep us from developing the courage we need to face grief. Many of us fear that, if allowed in, grief will bowl us over indefinitely. The truth is that grief experienced does dissolve. The only grief that does not end is grief that has not been fully faced.

Also, use the following ten signposts as a guide through the Valley of this Shadow of Death:

1. Cry
2. Scream
3. Shriek
4. Reach out to others
5. Reach into yourself
6. Sob
7. Take a deep breath
8. Whimper
9. Rest
10. Repeat the above as often as needed until you know that you'll make it through.

REFLECTION

Casper, Calla, Cajun, and Baxter

When I was growing up, my best friend was our dog, Sheba. She was three months older than I and was part of my life for as far back as I can remember. She was a great source of comfort and solace when my parents fought and argued. Sheba was as upset by it as I was, and the two of us used to hide in the closet of my room together. Sheba lived to be sixteen. Right up until the day I returned home from camp and my mother told me she had died, I just assumed she would always be around or even outlive me, the way some parrots outlive their owners.

I was hoping my thirteen-year-old Irish setter, Cajun, would hang on until this book was finished, but after we put down his mate, another Irish setter named Calla, he went downhill quickly. When I came back from a ten-day writing retreat in Vermont, I saw Cajun through new eyes. I realized then that he wasn't going to see me through to the end of the project as I'd hoped, and that it would be cruel to make him try.

I started making arrangements by phoning Mark, our veterinarian. I did not want to bring Cajun to the clinic. While Calla loved Mark, Cajun hated it there, and I didn't want his last act to be getting dragged somewhere he didn't want to go. Mark agreed to come to the house. The morning Mark was scheduled to arrive, Cajun did what every dog has a knack for doing in its last hour: he showed more signs of life than he had in three years. My first setter, Casper, my Irish soul mate, had done the same thing. On the morning he died, he was retrieving a tennis ball for my wife on only three legs (a broken hip caused the fourth to be taped to his side). He hadn't eaten in three days, as he could no longer keep anything down, not even water, but he ran down that ball like Andre Agassi charging the net for the championship point at Wimbledon. When I came home after burying Casper, my face and hands covered with dirt and mud, I collapsed heaving and sobbing into Dana's outstretched arms. I grieved his loss for years.

As we awaited Mark's arrival, Dana said she noticed the copy of Ira Byock's *Dying Well* I had been reading the night before. "Who knows more about death than you right now? You're helping Cajun die well, you're doing a good thing," she said.

I appreciated what she said and the tender way she said it, but the irony was not lost on me. All the research and knowledge about dying gained from writing a book inspired by my father's death was helping me create the perfect "end of life" for my Irish setter. My father wouldn't think it ironic at all. He loved our dogs. In fact, it was his dying wish to have his ashes scattered on Casper's grave.

So I dutifully headed off into the field to dig Cajun's final resting place.

Digging the hole, I hit slate, rock, and roots. This labor of love was fast becoming a major pain in the ass. It was another reminder that dogs, like people, tend to die the way they lived. We called Cajun our "stubborn little Irishman." He was a totally devoted and faithful companion whose one desire in life was to please his masters, so long as what they wanted was exactly what he felt like doing. I broke a ten-pound maul trying to get the hole deep enough. I decided to keep the handle and left the iron ax head in the grave—a fitting symbol of his time spent with us.

Cajun's passing was incredibly peaceful. His and Calla's were my first intimate encounters with death after Dad died.

When Calla had gently slipped away in Mark's office, her head resting comfortably on my lap, I asked him, "Where were you when my father was dying?" I actually like that part of putting an animal down. It's all the angst leading up to the decision that tears me apart.

My sons, Julian and Oliver, helped me lower Cajun into the ground and cover his body with dirt. We scattered Calla's ashes on top of him. Because she had died in winter, burying her in the ground would have been incredibly difficult. We hadn't known what we wanted to do with her ashes, so we had held on to them. Now we knew why. For twelve years the two had been inseparable. Now they were together again.

Soon after Cajun died, a client told me she had a great nine-month-old rescue dog named Baxter she was foster-sitting while the animal shelter tried to find him a permanent home. She said she understood if it was too soon, but was I interested in adopting the dog? I thought about it a moment. What I concluded was that I did not want to go through a long winter with the loud silence that fills a house used to the "click, clicking" and "pitter patter" of red paws on wood floors. I told her I was.

I arranged to take Baxter for an afternoon and see how he behaved with children and if he would be okay with our neighbor's horses. My now six-year-old son Julian is a total cat person (proving God does have a sense of humor) and Baxter, a pure-bred golden retriever, is a lot of dog.

But the kids loved Baxter. He had the same energy they did. Oliver wanted to know if he could stay. He wanted Baxter to sleep with him. Julian took him running and echoing Ollie's sentiments, asked if we could keep him. "Please Dad, please."

Watching the boys run around in circles after the bounding pup, I realized that their only experience with dogs had been getting yelled at: "Not too rough!" "Cajun may not like that!" "Be careful of his bad leg!" "Cajun is an old man now, you have to be gentle with him." Several weeks later, when I arrived home from work, I was greeted at the door by both boys shouting, "Daddy, Daddy, come quick, look, Baxter knows how to climb stairs!"

In short, they had spent most of their lives living with two invalid animals in need of palliative care. By comparison, Baxter is superdog. He's indestructible. Like the kids, he is a one-dog wrecking crew. They're a perfect match. Baxter is the new life eagerly waiting to jump through the portal created by Cajun's death.

Life goes on.

PART TWO

SHELTER FROM THE STORM

And if I pass this way again, you can rest assured
I'll always do my best for her, on that I give my
   word
In a world of steel-eyed death, and men who are
   fighting to be warm.
"Come in," she said,
"I'll give you shelter from the storm."

—BOB DYLAN

6

The Wishing Well

LESSONS ON WORK AND LOVE

As ONE ENTHUSIASTIC reviewer observed, in his five-minute masterpiece "Shelter from the Storm," Bob Dylan takes us on a journey of desolation and loneliness, destination and unconditional love. The song's themes of loyalty and gratitude, questioning and hard knocks, awe over innocence in a harsh world, and the price of holding the tension between all the opposites that collide over the dusty, rocky trail of life's journey are enough grist for any father-son relationship.

The chapters that make up this book's second part examine ways fathers provide shelter for their sons and how these activities and relationships can continue to provide them refuge in their grief. Unfortunately, for some there is only the promise of protection but never genuine safety; as the narrator in Dylan's song laments in a later verse, "Now there's a wall between us, somethin' there's been lost, I took too much for granted, got my signals crossed." However, even sons who couldn't take their father's love for granted may find in mourning a chance to remove some of the walls that separate them and begin a different kind of dialogue with the man.

. . .

Is there any activity we associate more with fathers than work? For many men, work is synonymous with shelter. It provides us a respite from life's uncertainties and the relational challenges of family life that always seem more chaotic and unpredictable than any crisis we experience on the job, no matter what our vocation.

After the death of their father, many men literally work through their grief. Grief needs a creative outlet. For many of us, work offers one. Furthermore, the completion of the mourning cycle can result in an outpouring of creative energy (as evidenced by this book you're holding in your hands). This kind of focused activity can be a welcome escape from the exhausting and painful work of mourning, and some men depend on it to great personal gain.

"Nothing is more dangerous than an idea when it's the only one you have" is advice I find myself giving to a lot of my male clients whose lives are out of balance because of how much time they're spending at the office or how much overtime pay they're accruing. But, while it's currently in vogue to speak of men's penchant for workaholism, for most men work is a source of passion and pride. It gives our life purpose and meaning. For a father, nothing makes this pursuit more meaningful than to have his son join him in this endeavor.

One of the most well-known father-son portraits and unforgettable moments in our nation's storied past is the photograph of John F. Kennedy Jr. watching his father's funeral procession. A three-year-old "John-John," as he was affectionately called, wearing shorts and a buttoned-up coat, is standing at attention, offering his father a sad farewell salute as the president's flag-draped coffin rides by.

However, another less haunting, though equally moving, picture of this famous father-son dyad is a photograph of the son playing in the Oval Office, darting to and fro under his father's desk and between his legs. It was part of a series. These were some of the first photographs of this sort released by the White House, and it was no accident they showed the president on the job, hard at work, his son at his feet, happily entertaining himself.

The intent was to use the media to show a more personal side of JFK that would allow people to project him into their living rooms so they could relate to their commander in chief the way they would to a member of the family or a close friend. But the other message implied, even at John-John's young age, is the passing of the torch. The myth of Camelot. The legacy will continue.

When a son takes up his father's vocation, it is viewed as the highest form of adulation he can demonstrate—a testament to the bond the two men share and a father's legacy. All fathers want to live on through something, and it gets more poignant as we become more anonymous in the world. If work is the most common way men try to achieve this feeling of immortality, regrettably, for many fathers, their sons' careers become their masterpieces. This is unfortunate, because, as important as it may seem at times, the work is beside the point.

Work is simply another way for fathers to teach their sons how to love.

Death of a Mason

Leonard Kupinski, a forty-three-year-old computer programmer, described a day during his childhood that he spent working on a backyard project with his father, Stan, a stonemason. When his dad told him what they were doing, Lenny became so excited he could barely contain himself. "A wishing well?! We're gonna have a wishing well in our backyard? That is so cool!" "You better not let your mother hear you say that," said his father. "Doesn't she like wishing wells?" asked Lenny. "She likes them just fine, so long as they're not in her backyard," said his dad.

Lenny stayed by his father's side for the rest of the day. He was like a shadow. They spent most of it driving back and forth between their home, one along a long row of ramshackle houses stretching beside the river, and the site of an old torn-down building where they loaded the trunk of his father's car with bricks.

Lenny lost track of how many trips they made. "Hurry, hurry," his father shouted as he dropped the last two bricks into the open trunk. "How many do you think that is?" Lenny asked him. "How about just getting in the car already," his father shot back.

Lenny had never seen the car ride so close to the ground; he almost had to step down into it. "I guess we did all right, huh?" his dad said with a mischievous grin. "We could build the Great Wall of China with what we got in here!" Lenny said, grinning back. They both laughed. They couldn't stop. They laughed so long and so hard that they forgot what they were laughing about. And then they remembered and laughed some more.

"You want to get something to eat?" asked Lenny's dad. "What?" answered Lenny. "Do you want to get something to eat?" repeated his father. "You mean at a restaurant?" said Lenny, sounding as if he were choking on a chicken bone. "No, at the brickyard. Yes, at a restaurant," his father quipped back. "Yeah, sure. I mean yes. Absolutely. Definitely. Something to eat would be good," Lenny replied, trying to hide his shock.

His father had asked him to go out to eat and he'd almost blown it, thought Lenny to himself. His father never stopped to do anything when he was working. And he was always working. Lenny didn't know when the man slept. For the longest time, he didn't think he did.

As they drove to the Quick Stop Diner, his father glanced at Lenny sitting next to him on the bench seat, watching him. Lenny registered his father's every movement. Lenny knew it made his father uncomfortable when he looked at him that way. Lenny's father adjusted the mirror, shaking his head with an amused look on his face as he did.

Lenny thought his father had caught him again, but he was only adjusting the rearview mirror. He studied his father's profile. The man gave off an air of such strength. For Lenny, this was just further confirmation of the rumors he'd heard about his dad being in a great battle in World War II. His father never spoke about it, and Lenny knew better than to ask. A son knows not to ask his father about certain things.

His father still kept his hair cut short like the pictures of him in uniform. He was a few pounds heavier, but his face was still shaven, his mouth had the same strong line, and his eyes were still keenly aware, only older. He sat erect, both hands on the wheel. His father had the biggest hands of any man he'd ever seen. Lenny hoped to have hands like that someday. You could build worlds with hands like those. And that's what he planned to do when he grew up—he was going to build things, just like his dad.

When they arrived at the restaurant, Lenny ordered three pieces of chicken and mashed potatoes with gravy, just like his father. They ate in silence as the waitress hovered nearby, smiling at the picture they made: father and son having dinner.

The next weekend they cleaned up the brick and laid out a wishing well. They worked on it every night until dusk. It only went three feet deep; it wasn't a real one. Lenny knew that. It was very ticky-tacky, but his father brought home some four-by-four posts to put a little roof on it; it even had a little bucket and handle. Lenny loved it.

One night they were in the yard working together. This time Lenny caught his father watching him. He felt so happy. He wanted so much to be like his father, just as every ten-year-old boy wants to be. Lenny's father watched with pride at the enthusiasm his son had for the bricks and the mortar, and the trowels, and the tools. He was good with them, too.

Just then Lenny—who was excitedly splashing mortar on brick—said, "Hey Dad, look at what I did." At that moment, his father turned to him and said, "Lenny, if you ever grow up to be a mason ... "

"Yeah, Dad, yeah?"

"I'll break both your arms."

It was such a shock to hear him say that. He had never heard his father use words like those before. But thirty years later, as Lenny sat recalling them in my office, he said that even as a young child he could feel the mixed emotion with which his father expressed them:

> I immediately knew he was saying, "I want something better for you." I mean, obviously, it was really hard, backbreaking work. But I think the subtext was that it was something about him—maybe that sadness that I think he always carried with him that there wasn't a lot to be proud of about what he was. I think people of that generation define themselves by their occupation. "What are you?" "I'm a mason." "Oh."

Stan and Lenny's interactions were evocative of Willy Loman's heart-wrenching exchanges with his sons in Arthur Miller's *Death of a Salesman*. In Miller's modern American classic, Willy is coming to grip with the fact that he is no longer the successful salesman he once was. Eventually, he must cope with his sons discovering his awful truth. But Willy's sons don't dream of success, they dream only of their father, even as Willy's hopes for them and himself come to a crashing halt.

The irony that Lenny's father turned on him while working on this particular project—that this shocking betrayal took place beside a wishing well—was not lost on Lenny. Freud said, behind every fear is a wish. Driving Stan's fear that Lenny might follow him into masonry was his wish for a better life for his son.

Regardless of what a father does for a living, it's not learning about masonry (or life) that keeps a son standing at his father's side. Like Lenny, most men are just happy to be in close proximity to their fathers, to admire the sweat and muscle, to just be part of the man's life. It's the connection they wish for.

The desire to be closer to his father influences a man in countless ways. Back and forth over the course of his life he is pulled between hardship, bordering on despair, and the dream of his father's rescue—for his father's offer of shelter from the storm.

The Road Trip

Lenny was sleeping in the basement of his father's house when he found out his father had died. Lenny had come to help his mother care for his dad, who was at a hospice facility nearby. Lenny's wife and children had joined him that weekend.

It was the middle of the night when the phone rang, and Lenny woke up in a pitch-black room. He stumbled out of the bed and whacked his foot on something while trying to find the receiver. He tried to feel his way through the dark without stepping on either of his sons, Charlie and Henry, who were sleeping on the floor beside him. He remembers, when he finally got to the phone, fearing the worst and then hearing it.

Stan's demise was fast, mercifully so, felt Lenny. One morning Lenny had received an alarming call from his father in Rochester. "Son, it's Dad. I just had a physical and my blood tests show I have leukemia. I'm going to have to be on medication, but I'll be okay." Lenny was upset but also relieved because his father's was a treatable form of cancer and the longevity that the doctors gave someone with that diagnosis still put his father well into his eighties.

Rochester is one of America's biggest little cities. Despite its size and tough climate, it has world-renowned doctors, and its hospitals are considered some of the best in the country. Nevertheless, Lenny knew that at that moment, Rochester was lacking the one thing his father needed most—a big league ballpark.

As James Thurber observed about the majority of American males of his generation, Lenny's father put himself to sleep every night by striking out the batting order of the New York Yankees. Lenny's father loved the sport of baseball. He was a huge fan. Growing up, Lenny had played Little League, and despite how hard his father worked, Stan never missed one of his son's games.

When Lenny was ten years old, his father promised to take him to a big league game, but his father kept having to postpone it because of work. Finally, when Lenny turned thirteen, his father made good on his promise and took him to Boston to see a Red Sox game.

It was an incredible weekend. Lenny had a fabulous time—laughing and joking the whole way with his father, and they got to see a great game, too. The Red Sox won the game, but Lenny and Stan were the big winners that day.

Lenny was a huge Cincinnati Reds fan. This was the seventies—the glory days of Johnny Bench, Pete Rose, Joe Morgan, and the Big Red Machine—and he followed the Reds intensely. But after that trip, Lenny decided that if the Reds were his favorite team in the National League, he now had an American League team: he was going be a Red Sox fan. So he kept following them.

Now it happened to be 1975, and wouldn't you know it—the Red Sox played the Reds in the World Series that year. "It was a magical summer and that trip was central to it; it was something Dad and I would talk about for the rest of our lives," said Lenny.

Even after Lenny grew up and started a family of his own, he and his dad continued their tradition of going to baseball games together. On one car trip to Milwaukee to watch the Red Sox play the Brewers, Lenny's father told him detailed stories about his own childhood. "I always knew my grandfather was a mean old codger, but I had no idea how physically abusive he was," said Lenny. Stan told him shocking stories of his father beating his mother and Stan and his brothers running down the street to get help.

So upon hearing the news of his father's illness, Lenny hung up the phone and arranged for the two of them to go to a baseball game together.

Six weeks later, Lenny made the six-hour drive to Rochester to pick up his dad for their road trip. When Lenny arrived, his father said, "Hey Lenny, look at this." Stan pulled up his sleeve and pulled back a bandage on his arm and showed Lenny the most ugly, unnatural, bruiselike thing he'd ever seen. It was otherworldly looking. It did not look good. And his father said it hurt a lot to touch. So, instead of taking his father to the ball game as he'd planned, Lenny drove his dad to the hospital.

The doctor took one look at Stan's arm and said, "Oh, that's gotta go." Lenny couldn't believe how relaxed his father seemed, it was such a contrast to the doctor's alarming tone. After the doctor left, his father put his shirt back on. Lenny looked on in shock at his father's frail body all tattooed with crosses from his radiation. Stan caught his son staring at him. As soon as their eyes met, Lenny looked away. He felt like the same gaping little boy who had helped his father load bricks into the trunk of his car twenty-eight years earlier.

Stan finished buttoning up his shirt. When he was done, he sighed. He was tired. He looked around for his jacket, but before Stan had a chance to ask his son for help, Lenny had already retrieved it and was holding it out for him. Stan slid an arm through one sleeve and then very delicately guided his other arm, the one with the bruise or whatever it was, very slowly through the other sleeve while his son held it perfectly still—just the way his father had taught him to hold a level when pouring a floor.

After his father's hands cleared both openings, Lenny pulled the garment up over his dad's shoulders. Lenny's movements were gentle yet deliberate. His father fumbled with the zipper. "Let me get that," said Lenny. He kneeled down in front of his father and carefully fastened the zipper. Looking down, Lenny noticed something he never had before. Lenny had his father's hands, which seemed strangely unfit and uncomfortable when holding something so small as a zipper.

Lenny's large hands guided the tiny clasp on its path up his father's torso. When he was finished, Lenny's eyes met his father's again. This time Lenny didn't look away. The two men froze, caught in each other's gaze. Then Lenny leaned over and kissed his father gently on the forehead. His father closed his eyes as if his son had just said a prayer and his entire body was saying "amen." When he opened them, he looked at Lenny and said, "Len, life is like baseball. Line drives are caught. Squibbers go for base hits. It's an unfair game."

Nine months later his father was dead.

Stan had a Merkel cell tumor. The surgeon who had examined his arm in the hospital that day removed the growth a week later and made the diagnosis. After learning about his father's condition, Lenny researched Merkel cell on the Internet. What he found wasn't encouraging. It's very rare. Rare means there's not a lot of treatment options. Not many cases; not many experiments.

Lenny was incredibly grateful for the remaining time he and his dad got to spend together, but he wouldn't have wanted his father to live a day longer than he did. Not the way his father suffered.

During those long months leading up to Stan's death, the two men didn't talk about Stan's illness or what was to come. Like a couple of big league pitchers hanging out in the bull pen, they were most content when their minds and bodies were at rest. A pitcher, as George Plimpton observed in another context, is happiest with his arm idle. He knows that as soon as he gets on the mound and starts his windup, he delivers himself to the uncertainty of the future.

Lenny's father was buried two days after he died. There was a gathering for just immediate family and relatives at the funeral home. Lenny and some of his cousins brought things to put into the casket. "Gifts for the afterlife," is how Lenny described them, "like the pharaohs buried inside the pyramids in Egypt."

Stan loved playing cards. Poker, gin rummy, and pinochle—you name it, he played it. So Stan's first gift from his nephew was a deck of playing cards—Bicycle (large print)—and a set of horseshoes, which was another favorite game.

His father also had ridden a motorcycle in his youth. He used to bike all over the country during the forties and fifties. Lenny laughed out loud imagining his father on his rig, but stopped abruptly just thinking about his father's decision to let his Harley go. When his father sold his bike, he sold a piece of himself along with it, a part of himself that he never got back. So someone put some Harley memorabilia inside the casket.

Finally, Lenny took a small round object out of his jacket pocket. Holding it reminded him of one of his dad's tools. Pick it up and you instantly know its purpose. He couldn't think of anything else that came any closer to ideal in utility and design.

Lenny placed the baseball in his father's hand.

R-E-S-P-E-C-T

At some point during his protracted illness, my father seemed more at home in the hospital than he did in his own house. One visit I brought him a portable CD player so we could listen to music together. The "boom box"—which was doing a good job of living up to its name—was perched precariously on the windowsill of his hospital room.

I was playing deejay. Dad was in bed propped up on some pillows. We were in our element. Dad let the music sink into his bones, where the medicine and cancer were busy fighting for top billing. Jimi, Janis, John, Paul, George, and Ringo were just some of the specialists consulting with him that morning.

"Oh baby, I'm really groovin' on this," he said. My father really used language like that. It was as if someone had frozen him in the sixties and then thawed him out later. He was the original Austin Powers.

"Who is this singing?"

"The Queen of Soul," I answered, handing him a plastic cup of water and a straw.

"Aretha, yeah, of course. Man, isn't she something," he said in a choked voice, and took a sip of the water. "Too bad I can't get stoned anymore."

"Denise could always bake some in brownies and you could eat them," I suggested innocently. Dad furrowed his brow as if he was contemplating some important question one of his

114

students had posed him. "Ahhh, now there's a thought!" he said, holding his index finger in the air and falling back on his pillow.

Aretha's song "Dr. Feelgood" gave way to her chartbuster "Respect"—which she's practically turned into a brand name—and I began to dance. Dad's eyes, and the rest of his face, danced along with me. I cracked a smile just imagining the rest of his body joining in.

I immediately found myself transported back to the gym of the Valley Road Middle School in Princeton. I don't know how I talked my father into chaperoning my sixth-grade dance, but nevertheless, there he was, donning a three-piece suit with lapels wider than a six-lane highway and sideburns to match, dancing in the middle of the gym floor. Well, sort of dancing. Dad threw one leg out in front of him like Chubby Checker doing the twist; then he just left it dangling there while the rest of his body was engaged in what can best be described as a Martha Graham modern dance number. It was scary.

Twenty-six years later, lying in his hospital bed, his body ravaged by cancer, my father's sense of rhythm was the only thing the disease hadn't taken (you can't lose what you never had). "R-E-S-P-E-C-T, Find out what it means to me ... R-E-S-P-E-C-T ..." Suddenly, the door opened. Dad and I froze. I dove for the music player, hitting buttons that said "Loudness" and "Bass Booster" before finding the one labeled "Pause."

"This is where it's all happening this morning," pronounced a congenial-looking African American man. He acted as if he hadn't walked in on anything more unusual than a nurse taking someone's temperature or a doctor looking over a patient's chart.

"Hiya, George!" my father greeted our unexpected visitor. "This is my son Jonathan." George was wearing a blue jumpsuit that had a red patch on the front pocket with the words "Environmental Services" sewn in black lettering across it.

"Uh, um, hi," I said, wiping the sweat from my brow.

"Don't turn it down on my account," said George. And so the concert resumed. Except this time I had a partner. While George got started in the bathroom, his mop joined me on the main floor. Bolstered by George's vote of confidence, I turned the volume louder—"R-E-S-P-E-C-T, Find out what it means to me!"—so that neither Dad nor I noticed when the door opened a second time, causing the music to spill out into the hallway.

"Just visiting the sick, but we can see this is not a good time for you, Mr. Diamond. We'll come back later!" shouted an elderly Jewish woman from Temple Israel standing just inside the door. Another woman, refusing to cross the threshold and looking even more nervous than her friend, poked her head around the corner to see if she could make out what was going on inside. What she saw was me frozen mid-step in the center of the room holding my string-haired companion, and Dad sitting up in bed, both arms raised over his head, fingers snapping. Dad and I stared where the two women had been standing before they disappeared out the door and then at each other, and burst out laughing. Dad's laughing spasm quickly turned into a coughing one, and soon he was coughing uncontrollably.

I turned down the music and went to refill his water glass.

7

Wittgenstein's Tigers

LESSONS ON FAITH AND HUMOR

I don't want to achieve immortality through my work. I
want to achieve it through not dying.

—WOODY ALLEN

SEVERAL YEARS AGO a client of mine who knew something about
my own experience found out his father had a terminal illness. In
our next session he expressed his fear that he wouldn't be able to
muster the emotional resources he needed to face this grievous
loss and be there for his father. "What's the most important qual-
ity a person must possess to make it through something like
this?" he asked. I didn't hesitate: "A sense of humor."

A survivor of the Holocaust once was asked what he and
others did when they first arrived at the death camps. He said,
"We told jokes." Having experienced a trauma unimaginable by
most, these men and women taught us that it is possible to suffer
and doubt for a lifetime, yet not lose the art of laughter.

If you can find the humor in something, you can survive it.

Socrates Meets the Sopranos

One day my father remarked to his hero, the philosopher Martin Buber, that Freud is reported to have answered a question concerning the meaning of life by saying: work and love. Buber laughed and said this was good, but not complete. He would say: work, love, faith, and humor.

This sort of badinage is not likely to uncover the meaning of life, but the terms "work," "love," "faith," and "humor" do go a long way toward describing what was needed to sustain a relationship with my father. One crucial omission from this list is courage—and when trying to appreciate what it took to survive my father's dying, courage had a cast that was particularly Jewish. Every tragedy we experienced seemed a test of our faith and a challenge to redemptive action.

During one of his stays at the hospital, Dad and I planned the first of several father-son vacations to the Jersey shore. At the time, the New Jersey coastline was not the first destination you would think of heading off to if you were a person with a compromised immune system. Mine was healthy and in good working order, and even I had my reservations. This was just around the period that all the "red bag" trash receptacles containing used syringes and other medical waste kept washing up on shore.

Because of the increased risk of infection, Dad was frequently under doctor's orders to stay out of the water, which, as he put it, was a real downer. Dad loved swimming, but even when grounded he didn't get depressed, as he could still engage in the other activities he was passionate about—running and, during the winter months, skiing.

I loved watching him take up his lumbering gait as he headed down the beach in a slow jog, his feet sounding like bass drums pounding the old planks that lined the boardwalk. He had an endless supply of energy and a dogged determination to finish the race. He did not want to die a sick and helpless man, and as a result, he refused to surrender to the aches and pains of his tired and battered body. If the doctors told him he couldn't swim, he'd ski. If he couldn't ski, he'd run. If he couldn't run, he'd walk.

We stayed at an old bed-and-breakfast in Spring Lake with views of the ocean and lots of nooks and crannies to sit in, enjoying a hot or cold drink while getting lost in a good book. Unfortunately, there wasn't going to be much leisure reading for me on this trip. I had just started my dissertation, a huge undertaking, which eventually became my first book. In the evenings, while I toiled away writing, Dad busied himself playing games of chance inside one of Atlantic City's palatial casinos.

These trips created many lasting memories, but they didn't make miracles. Rather, given our history, the miracle was that we were able to make them happen at all. Even though he was full of the best intentions, Dad was still capable of lashing out in crazy, unpredictable ways that seemed lifted straight from the pages of an Augusten Burroughs story. After fourteen years in Al-Anon and nine more in therapy, it was still all I could do not to become reactive.

One morning after informing my father that I was going to go to the gym before breakfast, I watched him try his hardest not to get agitated. He was failing wonderfully.

"Why don't you work out after we eat?" Dad asked innocently enough.

"Because I want to exercise before breakfast. If you need to eat sooner, you go ahead. I'll catch up to you later and we can go to the beach," I said. I worried Dad might sense that I was trying too hard to sound reasonable and feel patronized.

"I don't feel like eating alone. It's depressing," he said in a sullen tone.

"Well, then wait. I won't be long," I responded, trying to placate him.

"Look, you know how I feel about eating late, and this is the kind of place that makes all the food at one time. If we wait, the food is going to get cold. Why didn't you get up earlier if you knew you wanted to write and work out before breakfast?!"

His voice had the same high-pitched edge and forced restraint he had used when talking to our mother when I was a child—like an acerbic opera singer trying to hit a high C. It was the kind of sound that, when sustained over time, breaks dishes.

I was starting to strategize what my next move would be when, without warning, Dad pulled out a syringe and, with the same nonchalance he might use to adjust the waistband of his boxer shorts, injected himself in the thigh with Procrit. Dad looked no more alarmed than he would if he were applying Icy Hot to his knees before going for a run.

I was in shock. Suddenly, I realized this conversation was ending. One day very soon, we wouldn't be fighting like this. "You let me have first dibs on the sports section and I'll work out before lunch," I said as we headed down to breakfast.

Over breakfast, we talked about the killing he had made at the blackjack table the night before (or so he said) and the progress of my latest chapter. Dad read what I had written the previous day and returned it to me, his comments and suggestions penned across the page in his barely legible scrawl. He was my toughest critic and my biggest fan.

Philosophy as Therapy

At my father's memorial service, one of his students said that her older sister had told her, "When you get to Princeton you have to take a course with Mal Diamond. Professor Diamond will crawl up the walls if it helps to make his point." During my father's forty-year career of teaching, Austrian-born philosopher Ludwig Wittgenstein was responsible for more claw marks on the walls of my father's classrooms than any other thinker he taught.

A son who has just received his Ph.D. tells his Jewish mother his great news: "Ma, I'm going to become a doctor of philoso-phy!" His mother replies, "That's wonderful! So tell me, what kind of disease is philosophy?" Wittgenstein would approve of this story, as he viewed philosophy as sick and in need of treat-ment. He intended his grammatical and philosophical investiga-tions as a kind of therapy.

Talking philosophy with my father wasn't good therapy for me. In fact, it didn't resemble anything even remotely therapeu-tic. Engaging him in a conversation about philosophy—preparing for it, engaging in it, decompressing from it—was more like my run with him to the store for ketchup. Same rhythm. Same out-of-body-like feelings of disassociation. Same gratitude for arriving (sort of) in one piece (sort of). Same wondering whether there's any adult in the room.

Nevertheless, those of us who forget history are able to enjoy it more when we repeat it. So it was with great enthusiasm, on one of our walks along the boardwalk at Spring Lake, that I asked my father if the particular way I was employing Wittgen-stein's ideas in my dissertation was even remotely close to any-thing the great philosopher intended.

After I posed the question, I held my breath and waited for his answer. Dad didn't need that much time. My eyes began glaz-ing over and my head started hurting as my father, who was just starting to rev up, proceeded to set me straight.

"Oh I think I get it now, Dad," I said, cutting him off and launching into an explanation of my own. "Is that it, Dad?" I asked when I'd finished.

"No, that's not quite it," my father responded, trying to dis-guise his impatience. "Listen," he said, visibly annoyed by the interruption and readying himself to launch into a lecture I'd attended many times before and simply called "Explaining complex philosophical concepts to ungrateful son without the educational background to understand what the hell I'm talking about." But before continuing his tutorial, he did a double take.

Then he raised one eyebrow and with a look of disbelief and amazement said, "Actually, that's exactly it!"

I was dumbfounded. My astonishment quickly gave way to jubilation. It's hard to imagine a philosopher like Wittgenstein or even one of lesser stature engaging in the sort of celebration pro football players perform in the end zone after scoring a touchdown. Yet somehow, dancing backward in the sand in front of where my father was standing, with my hands held over my head, shouting "Yes, *yes*, YES!" felt very . . . well . . . very right.

When I dropped to my knees, looked up at the sky, and began beating my chest in the fashion of a European soccer player after scoring a goal, the expression of amused surprise on my father's face turned to one of exasperation and anger. "Come on, Dad," I chided in the most consoling tone I could muster. "I've been waiting my whole life for this day to come, this is my Oedipal moment of truth!" "I know," he responded in his most nebbishy, dear-old-dad voice. "That's the problem—it's mine too."

Dad had a knack for taking moments like this—infused with the thrill of victory and the agony of defeat—and making them more poignant. And making them more about him as well, I suppose.

In my father's world, celebration never crowded out mourning and mourning was always an opportunity to celebrate. This particular exchange on the beach marked the beginning of a new intellectual bond between us, one we maintained right up until (and beyond) his death.

For me, our conversation along the shore and the reconciliation it engendered were about my coming to terms with a subject my father had always been an authority on and the way he used it to wield a certain kind of power over my life. More important, it was an acknowledgment of the ways both my parents had contributed to my development and the person I was becoming. Growing up, this type of perspective had been hard to come by. Moving closer to my father and his interests was, developmentally speaking, no easy task to accomplish. And because of his violent temperament, it was often a dangerous one. Like trying to cuddle up with a Tyrannosaurus rex who loves you a lot (sort of).

It was during times like these that our humor served us most. Laughter helped Dad and me create a safe space where we could use our creative imaginations to, borrowing analyst Christopher Bollas's term, "crack up" the seemingly fixed stories and immovable objects in our relationship and replace them with more affirming and less destructive ones.

What was noteworthy about that particular conversation with my father at Spring Lake—and all the time we spent together at the shore—was the way it conspired to change my perception of him. No, it was more than that. This exchange didn't just change my perception of my father or my father's perception of me; it changed my perception of my father's perception of me. It changed how we chose to be together in the present, how we related to large parts of our past, and how we planned to be in our future.

Freud talked of children grappling with Oedipal experience somewhere between the ages of three and five, but speaking for myself (a pretty typical Jewish son), I see completion of this developmental task as taking place somewhere between the ages of thirty and fifty. While every son's experience may differ and my math may be a little fuzzy, my point is that this dance of intimacy between child and parent—with its moves of intense closeness, extreme distance, and everything in between—continues throughout the life cycle.

The relational aspects of these developments are—as so many feminist writers, thinkers, and therapists remind us—what Freud missed with his one-way accounts of therapy and love. It doesn't work that way. Sometimes I move others. Sometimes another moves me. It's a dynamic process. Oedipal love is always a two-way street. Whether both parties are blinded by it or can plainly see it, the two are bound together by fate.

Dad found his own way of letting me in on that little secret and sharing how much my moving closer to his world meant to him. Now that I'm a father myself, I realize what a humble and vulnerable position that was for him (or any parent) to be in. This kind of give-and-take, no matter how late in life we came by it, was a precious gift for both of us.

Anything We Love Can Be Saved

How we got there remains somewhat of a mystery to me. Sometimes a solution is so obvious that we cannot see it, even though it is right before our eyes. According to my father's favorite thinker, Wittgenstein, what we need in those moments is to learn to assemble what "already lies open to view."

Maybe, without fully understanding it, this is exactly what I did. To cure my haunting sense of loss and bridge my father's world and mine, I did not reach so much for deep analysis or subtle explanations of what was happening to us. Instead, I turned to something much more mundane and much more open to view.

I went shopping for CDs.

At the time of my "classic rock attack," I hadn't bought any new music since my first son, Julian, had been born five years earlier. Consequently, I had no trouble rationalizing a hundred-dollar shopping spree at my local music store. When I came home and began taking my purchases out of the bag, I suddenly realized that I'd brought home all the albums my father and I used to play together. We'd listen to them for hours, sitting on the living room floors of the apartments he lived in following my parents' divorce— the one on University Place and later on Bayard Lane.

It was hard-driving music that pushed thoughts of anything but the beat from your mind: the Rolling Stones, *Let It Bleed* and *Sticky Fingers*; Traffic, *The Low Spark of High Heeled Boys*; the

Beatles, *Magical Mystery Tour* and *Let It Be*; Cream, *Disraeli Gears*; Bob Dylan, *Highway 61 Revisited*; Joe Cocker, *With a Little Help from My Friends*; The Doors, *Strange Days*; Jimi Hendrix, *Are You Experienced?*; and Janis Joplin, *Cheap Thrills*, *I Got Dem Ol' Kosmic Blues Again*, and *Pearl* (Dad loved Janis).

We played them over and over again, the grooves in the vinyl worn down like patches of fur on the Velveteen Rabbit. Sometimes the music was the only thing we could relate to or talk about with one another. The songs were for us what box scores and baseball represented for Lenny and Stan and so many other fathers and sons. It was a way of calling over the fence, so to speak, which at times was the only safe intimacy we could tolerate. It allowed us to connect.

When I was twelve or thirteen, I gave Dad a birthday present—a sky blue T-shirt with the words "Wittgenstein Tigers" in white lettering emblazoned across the front. It was, beyond a doubt, the most excited I'd ever seen my father become over a gift he'd received from me. "I love it, Wus!" he exclaimed, using his pet name for me. "I can't wait to show it to the group," he added, referring to a seminar he was teaching that included some of his favorite students. Then he leaned over, pulled me close, and gave me a huge kiss and a bad case of razor burn to go along with it.

I loved those kisses.

At bedrock there was always a strong bond between us. That was never in doubt. But, borrowing another one of my father's intellectual hero's expressions, what if I've been using the wrong kind of "language game" to unlock the mysteries of our relationship? What if I've been looking to philosophers for answers when I should have been turning to poets?

Even before I had a clue who Wittgenstein was, I could see he was taking up way more space in my father's head than he was paying rent for. He was part philosophical muse, part intellectual

tormentor, and I saw how exuberant my father became when trying to explain him to students. I identified with the fierce loyalty
the philosopher inspired in him and the mix of joy and anguish
this caused my father.

Recently, I read a passage in which one of Wittgenstein's former students at Cambridge described the philosopher's temperament as being akin to an atomic bomb or a tornado. He said he
felt total adoration in his teacher's presence or felt struck dumb
with sheer terror, and often a combination of the two. Like his
intellectual mentor, my father was tortured by what he understood to be his moral shortcomings and took his frustrations out
on the people he was closest to and who loved him the most.

I've always felt my life more resembled Alice Walker's title
Anything We Love Can Be Saved than it did the dense writing of
Wittgenstein, Buber, and the other philosophers my father, as he
so quaintly put it, "grooved on." But as the cliché goes, "Love is
not always enough." And it wasn't for Dad and me, either. We
needed something more.

I think these objects—the records, the T-shirt, my childhood
artwork that hung on the walls of his office—and others like
them served as reminders that no matter how confused or mud-
dled things became between us, if we were willing to abandon
our quest to try to solve or fix the problems we faced (or each
other), everything would become easier. We started making
headway when we stopped trying to resolve our many contradic-
tions and just tried to get a clear view of them.

Our fit was more like the jagged edges of the dramatic rock
formations found along the Continental Divide than the exact-
ness or kind of perfection one experiences when resting a
machine-sewn hardball inside the pocket of a well-oiled baseball
glove. Yet even with all its flaws and imperfections, there was a
certain grace to our relationship.

"It is clear great flyers have always been great fallers," writes
Sam Keen in his *Learning to Fly*, a collection of philosophical

reflections on the trapeze, fear, trust, and the joy of letting go. In a story Keen recounts in his book, one of the early legendary flying acts of the century was composed of Earnest Clarke, the flyer, and Charles Clarke, the catcher. Without any third person to return to the trapeze, these brothers mastered a double somersault and a pirouette return. Keen quotes an interview from Irving Pond's *Big Top Rhythms* during which Pond asked Ernie about falling:

> "Ernie, you must have had a few falls into the net before you got that act to perfection. Five hundred, say?"
>
> "Well," he answered, "five hundred would hardly be a circumstance. We tried it at each and every rehearsal for a year and no fewer than ten times at each rehearsal before ever our hands came together (and every try meant a fall into the net). Then we caught and held. In three and a half years more we reached the point where we thought we would be justified in presenting it in public. More than two thousand falls; and then three and a half years before it was perfected."

The transformation from angry nemesis to loving parent and angry young man to grateful son was, for my father and me, hard-earned. It did not happen overnight. There was no epiphany. There was a lot of falling.

It was the accumulation of hundreds if not thousands of little reminders captured in the lyrics and harmonies of a nostalgic song, the wording on a tattered article of clothing, or a child's faded artwork. Collectively, these moments—gifts of the heart—served as a relational hope chest where the most precious parts of ourselves could be stored for safekeeping.

The Race

My father and I were at one of my brother's high school football games. They were playing Trenton, at Trenton. Dad and I were horsing around on the asphalt track that encircled the playing field. Waiting for the teams to come out to start the second half of the game, we decided to race. First person to complete one lap around the track wins.

Dad began slowly and steadily, using the lumbering horse stride he was (in)famous for. Always slow out of the blocks, Dad was deceptively fast. The more distance involved, the more likely he was to make it up and close the gap between you and him, which is why I took little comfort from any advantage I enjoyed.

At the race's beginning we started out right next to each other, and for the first fifty or sixty yards we stayed locked in that position. After the first turn I started building up more of a lead, which, as we moved into the backstretch, I tried to build on. Approaching the second turn, I was feeling better than usual. This was where, customarily, I would start to tire and Dad gained strength. But today I felt as if I was running with the wind. I listened for my father's gallop, sure he was just toying with me and waiting for me to collapse in a heap as he sailed past me. I couldn't hear him.

Coming out of the final turn, I looked over my shoulder to find out how much fuel I would need in my tank in order to fend

Dad off at the end. I couldn't see him. I looked farther back; to my astonishment, he hadn't even entered the final turn. Shortly after, he gave up altogether, and I heard him shouting at the top of his lungs *"Go, Wus!"* as he waved me on ahead. I raced down the homestretch to the finish line, toward a victory that I'd waited for the entire thirteen years of my life.

Dad began to walk off the track. At first, I thought he was hurt or had thrown the race to make me feel better, but as soon as I caught up to him I could tell neither was the case. "Why did you quit?" I asked, trying not to sound too triumphant but also genuinely concerned. "You can run harder than that." "I'm running twice as hard as I ever did. I'm just not getting there as fast," Dad answered with a grin.

I'll never forget the look on my father's face at that moment. It was irrepressible joy and elation and profound sadness and disappointment all at the same time. Whatever that emotion is, that's the look I saw on my father's face.

I think this is what Freud was getting at when he said that Oedipal victories are, for every son, both a celebration and a murder. Winning, in this instance, is bittersweet, because every race won, every tool mastered, every degree earned, every book written or business deal successfully negotiated brings us closer to our father's death and the conclusion of whatever sort of partnership we've enjoyed and endured with the man.

8

What Was He Thinking!?!

LESSONS ON VIOLENCE AND REDEMPTION

God said to Abraham, "Kill me a son."
Abe said, "Man, you must be puttin' me on."
God said, "No." Abe said, "What?"
God said, "You can do what you want, Abe, but . . .
Next time you see me comin', you better run."
Abe said, "Where do you want this killin' done?"
God said, "Out on Highway 61."

—BOB DYLAN

THE BOY STUMBLED. The sun's rays reflecting off the sand and rocks temporarily blinding him, his knee scraped the ground, its skin cut open on the gravelly surface. It stung when the air hit it. He almost dropped the heavy load he was carrying but quickly regained his balance and continued up the slope. It was hot. His throat was dry and his feet, accustomed to strenuous walking over parched, hard land, were sore and starting to burn. He had been walking all morning and although they had no particular time they had to be there—wherever "there" was—the boy felt pressured to hurry. It was hard keeping up. His father took one long stride for every two of his.

Hundreds, thousands of thoughts raced inside the child's head—and just as many questions. Some obvious: Where were they going? Why were they doing this? What was their hurry? Who awaited them atop the mountain? And some less evident: Why was his father so quiet? There was heaviness about him the son had never witnessed before. Why was he being so mysterious about what they were going to do? They had performed similar rituals many times before.

Finally he could no longer contain himself: "Father, here are the firestone and the wood; but where is the sheep for the burnt offering?" "God will see to the sheep for his burnt offering, my son." They arrived at a large clearing near the top of the mount. "We will build it here," his father said. Isaac set about building an altar while his father arranged the wood. "Isaac," his father said in a commanding but gentle tone, "I need you to lie atop the altar, my son." "I don't understand, Father." "Trust me, Isaac. I love you more than life itself. I would never do anything to cause you harm." But the son sensed a quaver in the father's voice as he spoke these last words.

Isaac obeyed his father and lay down on the altar. When he stretched his body out its full length, his hands and feet hung awkwardly over the sides of the makeshift structure. His father methodically wrapped the cords around his arms, legs, and neck, and pulled hard. The ropes became taut. Isaac felt the breath leaving his body. His father checked the tightness of the cords, his fingers trembling, fumbling over the knots. They were much tighter than Isaac expected. If Abraham was going to have to go through with it, he wanted it to be over quickly. He did not want to miss or make a mistake. The boy shouldn't feel any pain or suffer needlessly.

When the father finished, the son couldn't move his limbs or turn his head. He could only see what was directly in front of or above him. Isaac stared up into his father's expressionless eyes. He almost didn't recognize him. It was as if his father had gone somewhere else and someone or something else had taken him over and inhabited his father's body. "Be still, my son." Even his voice sounded different. As if he were speaking to him from far away.

Moving only his eyes, Isaac tried to look around. A hill rose above them to his right. The sky was a brilliant blue. There was nothing in it to shield his naked eyes from the sun's blinding light. Isaac's temples started to throb. Ropes digging into his flesh, his head feeling as if it might split open any minute, he thought he was going to retch.

Just then his father pulled a long, thin, shining silver knife from inside his robes. Abraham gripped the blade very tightly in his right hand. A second later, Isaac realized what his father was about to do. He closed his eyes tightly and tried to cry out, but no sound came from his open mouth. Abraham swung his arm holding the knife above his head and prepared to slay his son.

What was he thinking!?!

That is both my reaction and my response. And of course, that's the sixty-four-thousand-dollar question: What was Abraham thinking?

The story of Isaac and Abraham functions as a kind of touchstone for all modern father-son relations. According to the Hebrew Bible, the patriarch was given a promise by God—not a promise of personal immortality but a promise that he would live on through his offspring and that the extended family of his descendants would become a great nation.

It does not concern me whether Abraham actually heard the voice of God or was carrying out the Lord's instructions. I have no way of knowing this and no way of finding it out; although one thing I'm pretty certain of is that had the Lord asked a mother to make the same sacrifice, God would still be waiting. What interests me is what it has to tell us about fathers and sons and the kinds of stories we choose to tell about them—and especially about the challenges it poses to a son grieving his father's death.

From the standpoint of fathering, I view Abraham's offering of Isaac as a father's attempt to prepare his son for a violent world and to initiate his son into a world of violence. For me, it is a metaphor that gives fathers license to abuse and traumatize their sons in order to prepare them for life and help them survive it.

I reject the notion that in order for a boy to become a man, he must endure great suffering at the hands of his father. Nevertheless, I understand the sort of devotion Abraham exhibits to a force that is both terrifying and embracing. It elicits something very primitive, an unwavering loyalty to a person or entity that can (with the same hand) either elevate or obliterate you. It is an odd mix of love and fear.

Jesse: An Invitation to Compassion

My eleven-year-old client Jesse was having difficulty sitting comfortably in his chair and was visibly ill at ease. He was participating in a group that I facilitated for children at his school. Jesse had been referred to me by his teachers because he was experiencing "family troubles."

He was reluctant to speak to me at first, but after encouragement from other members of the group, Jesse lifted his shirt to reveal a huge welt on his back and a nasty-looking black-and-blue contusion surrounding it. It looked painful. Jesse told me his father had punched him in his back and thrown him against a wall during an argument at home. Jesse was both relieved and concerned when I explained to him that I was required by law to file a child abuse complaint, and that in this instance I would have done so whether I was required to or not.

Jesse was not the only one troubled by this turn of events. Jesse's father had a reputation for explosive violence, and his mother pleaded with me not to file the child abuse report. Although she told me her husband had thrown a beer can at her the same evening he struck Jesse, she assured me that things had been improving.

I had tried for months to get Jesse's father to participate in the family counseling sessions. Reporting Gere for child abuse was not how I wanted to launch our therapeutic relationship, so I decided to send him a letter in the hopes it would be an opportunity to connect with him.

Its contents explained that because I was a mandated reporter of child abuse I had to make a report to the Department of Social Services. I wrote that I knew how much he loved his children, which was evident even from the brief contact we'd had, but that I did not think he could live with himself if any serious physical injury or harm came to any of them as a consequence of his behavior.

> Jesse's recollection of your apology to him also speaks to your consciousness of the emotional and spiritual damage that results when your anger escalates to physical violence and is directed toward others.
>
> Please call me as soon as possible so that we can talk about any options and resources that are available to help that you may not be aware of. I know you have been trying hard to manage your feelings safely. Although over time there has been some improvement, it is my sense recently that things are getting worse instead of better, and desperately need tending to.

The day he received my letter, Gere called my office to set up an appointment.

I am not a person who moves through the world with a lot of fear. I am not a small man. I work out a lot. However, a few minutes before our appointment, I did something I had never done before. I told the office manager about my upcoming session and left my door ajar. My anxiety was short-lived. With the letter I'd sent him resting in his lap, Gere acknowledged his anger at me about what had happened, but like his son, he was also clearly relieved. He spent most of the session talking about his relationship with his own father.

Gere said his father was a brutal man who used to torture him. For entertainment, his father used to make Gere run laps around their dairy farm until he peed in his pants while his father sat on the fence drinking beer and shouting obscenities at him. For punishment, he used to make his son dig ditches the length of his body. He'd tell Gere that he was digging his own grave and that he could postpone the inevitable as long as he kept shoveling dirt. And Gere, believing his father capable of anything, wouldn't stop until he collapsed from exhaustion or his mother came out to rescue him.

Against his mother's protests, Gere's father shipped him off to a military academy—the same one his grandfather had sent his dad to.

Gere's first years at the academy were tough but not as hard as they were on some. The hazing the older boys and the upper classmen put the younger ones through was terrifying. While other boys were reduced to tears and considered quitting, Gere was unfazed. His father's brutal treatment of him had prepared him well for what he faced at the military school.

Gere doesn't remember exactly when it happened, but at some point during his training he decided that there were two types of men in this world: the ones who were forced to run laps until they peed in their pants, and the ones sitting on the fence shouting orders and laughing at them. He committed himself to making sure that he fell in the latter category. This experience, coupled with his father's violent and erratic outbursts, scarred him deeply. At some point he found that alcohol numbed the pain.

Then something happened that caught Gere off guard. His father started treating him differently, taking more interest in his son's activities and telling Gere he was going to make his old man proud.

Basking in this newfound attention, Gere tried hard to please his dad. In college, he was captain of all his sports teams and at his father's urging joined ROTC. In fact, many of his friends criticized him because he cared too much about his father's opinions and showed no interest in trying anything that his father didn't approve of first.

Sports wasn't the only thing Gere excelled at in college. Gere's drinking had just started to become a problem when he met Nelly, whom he would later marry. Nelly convinced Gere to straighten up and focus more on his studies, which he did. When they graduated, the two wed, and after fulfilling his obligation to the military, Gere began a very successful career as a civil engineer. He went to night school for his masters and eventually started his own consulting firm.

He had three children, a large home, two expensive cars, and a dog. He'd accomplished all his goals and had everything he wanted.

When his father died, Gere told me, he felt incredible relief. Gere loved his father and wanted to remember the good things he had taught him, but he also felt as though something inside him changed. It was as if someone had flipped a switch. He was angry all the time. He became short-tempered with the kids at home and with his associates at work.

The hardest thing for him was parenting. The year Gere's dad died, Jesse turned eleven—the age Gere had been when he was sent away to the military academy—and Gere began to hate him. Before that, his favorite thing in life had been spending time with his son. Now he found himself growing furious at him for the smallest things. It wasn't anything in particular that Jesse was doing or not doing that made him mad; it was his son's carefree nature. He thought Jesse was lazy, and just looking at him made his blood boil.

Jesse was an excellent student. But while he took his schoolwork seriously, he also liked doing the sorts of things every eleven-year-old boy enjoys. He loved to daydream, skateboard, play computer games, listen to music, and hang out with his friends. In short, Jesse wasn't doing anything wrong, he was just being a kid. Gere resented his son terribly because when he was Jesse's age, he wasn't allowed to play. When he was home, he was expected to behave like an adult. When he was at the academy, he was expected to behave like a soldier.

Gere and I had several more sessions together, as well as one with Nelly, but by far, the most effective meetings were a series of visits that Gere and Jesse, now twelve, attended together. In these father-son sessions we began the painstaking work of unpacking the legacy of family violence that had been handed down from Gere's grandfather to his dad, from Gere's dad to him, and now from Gere to Jesse.

Gere had always worshipped his dad, but his growing realization of his father's cruel treatment of his wife and son enraged him. "He never really gave a damn about us. His only concern was where his next drink was coming from," he declared in one of our conversations. Gere promised himself at a very young age that he would never have a son who felt that way about him. Now that his worst fear appeared to have come to fruition, it was hard for him not to feel like a failure.

Slowly, with lots of guidance and patience, Gere began to understand that his anger wasn't about his son and him. It was about his father and him.

Whenever Gere tried to be different with Jesse, he said, he heard the voices of all the men in his family saying, "You're going to make him soft. Do you want to turn your son into a sissy?"

During one of our meetings, I asked Gere if he could come up with an image to help us understand why it was so difficult for him to act differently with his own son.

"Close your eyes for a moment and paint me a picture," I said.

Gere sat back in his chair, eyes closed, his thick hands folded neatly on his lap, and breathed deeply.

Gere described a chorus of men going back generations, all of them standing in uniform shouting orders at him.

"What would need to happen in order for you to silence or rid yourself of these voices?" I asked.

Tears started streaming down his face. "It would mean having to accept that my own father never tried to protect me from his anger the way I need to shelter Jesse from mine," said Gere.

Following this session Gere, Jesse, and I met on three more occasions. This resulted in the most dramatic and sustained improvement in Gere's abusive behavior and drinking habits in years.

Writing about Gere's mistreatment of Jesse was very hard for me. Many of the men I see in my practice offer similar accounts of neglect, abuse, and abandonment. Men who suffer this type of treatment from their fathers may unconsciously repeat these patterns with their own children. In many cases, it is the only way they have of remembering or memorializing their fathers. Legacies of hurt and pain are passed down like birthrights from one generation to the next.

All Men Are Sons

In my work with sons like Jesse or fathers like Gere, it is easy for me to lose faith. It is hard to avoid my clients' despair that nothing they do will make any difference. I try not to give in to their sense of hopelessness, but some days I feel resigned to this cycle of abuse continuing for generations.

As a young therapist, I tried to resolve this dilemma by putting clients like Jesse in untenable positions. My efforts to protect them from their fathers' rages and effect some kind of positive change would push them into making an impossible choice between their fathers and a safe and healing relationship with me in therapy.

What I learned is that when faced with such a choice, 99 percent of the time my clients would settle for the safety of parental approval no matter how abusive or neglectful their parent had been. Put another way, as David Treadway, a colleague, an author, and a family therapist is fond of saying, "Blood is thicker than therapy."

As a result of my work with Jesse and his father, my goals for therapy are much humbler now. I no longer try to rescue my clients, even those recovering from the effects of physical or sexual abuse and other kinds of emotional and psychological torture. Barbara Kingsolver said, "The least we can do with our lives is to find what it is we hope for. The most we can do is try to live inside that hope." Therapists are purveyors of hope.

What hope is there for men like Jesse and Gere and those of us who have had similar experiences? There is a popular expression: "What doesn't kill you makes you stronger." The assumption is that while it's awful living through events like these, surviving them leaves us changed for the better. This misses the point. It's not that the injury changes us for the better, it's that our understanding of the injury changes us for the better.

In relationships marred by violence, it is a son's love for his father—not his anger—that causes him to hate the man. It is the betrayal that hurts most. The physical wounds heal, but the emotional scars remain. Mourning a violent and abusive father is an act of defiance and of hope.

Men like Gere and sons like Jesse, Randy, and Craig (my clients whose letters to their dads were shared in chapter 5) are what Terry Real calls "relational heroes," because when faced with the prospect of their own grief and violence, each one refused to go down into that dark vortex with his father. But neither—as Real writes about—did they let go of their fathers' firm embrace.

An Unholy Alliance

In 1965 our family spent the year in Oxford, England. I was five years old. It was suppertime and my parents were in the middle of an argument. My father was brooding in silence at his usual spot at the head of the table. My brother was sitting across from me. Mom had just finished bringing the food out when my dad asked my brother to pass him something.

To this day, I don't know what my brother said in response. What I do remember is my father leaping out of his seat and lunging at my brother. "Goddamn it, Michael!" he screamed, and grabbed my brother's throat. The two of them spilled over the back of my brother's chair onto the hardwood floor. My father, his hands still wrapped around my brother's neck, continued to shout and swear at him.

By this time my mother was standing over them. "Stop it, Malcolm, stop it, you're choking him!" she yelled, pounding with her fists on his back and shoulders. "You're going to kill him!" she sobbed, pulling on his arms, hair, and shirt—anything she could get hold of. What seemed like hours was probably over in less than a minute, thirty seconds even.

Dad released his grip.

When my mother picked my brother up off the floor, he was red-faced and crying, although he tried not to show it. Dad was panting, his hair tousled; he had a wild look in his eyes and wore an expression on his face that was a mix of anger, shame, and what I can only call lunacy. He seemed crazed.

My mother asked my brother if he was all right. He didn't say anything. "Are you all right?" she repeated. "I'm fine," he answered, staring at our father in disbelief and, no doubt, asking himself, *What was he thinking!?!* Then rubbing his neck and looking more than a little dazed, he ran upstairs to his room.

"You broke the chair," my mother said, turning toward my father. But before she could utter another sentence he picked up his plate and silverware and retreated to his study. My mother stood in stunned silence, staring at the empty seat my father had just abandoned.

"Are you okay?" she asked without looking at me. I opened

my mouth and tried to answer her, but no sound came out. I tried once more and managed an "Uh, huh," while nodding my head up and down. "I'm gonna go see Michael," I said, and without waiting for her response I bolted from the table.

That was one of my earliest encounters with Dad's violent temper and how utterly terrifying and frightening he could be when he turned it on you. And what an unpredictable and scary place the world could become as a result.

Throughout my life, my brother served as a kind of "human shield" between my father and me. I've long felt that as a result of this sacrifice, I walked away from our home life relatively unscathed, which at times has resulted in my experiencing intense bouts of survivor's guilt. Whether because of his having absorbed more of our father's awful rage or because he had a constitution that was more vulnerable to it, my brother suffered terribly from Dad's violence in ways I never did.

The fact that something is a joint experience doesn't mean it's a similar one. The last time my father hit me I was six, maybe seven, years old. We were driving home to Princeton from a family gathering in New York City. My brother and I were carrying on in the backseat. After issuing several warnings, my father swung his arm from one side of the car to the other, like a back-hand smash on a tennis court. I think he was aiming for the side of my head, but I must have been leaning back in an effort to make him miss and so the full force of the blow struck my eye. I saw stars and then everything went dark.

"My eye, my eye, my eye!!!" I screamed. My mother pulled over onto the shoulder. I ran out of the car, squeezed my tiny body through the gates of a chain-link fence that separated the highway from an abandoned parking lot, and hid beside the wall of a large building. My mother gave chase but could go no farther than the fence. Eventually she coaxed me back to the car. Except for my crying, we sat in silence for the remainder of the trip.

When our Citröen rolled to a stop in the driveway of our home at 393 Walnut Lane, I fled to my room. My mother tried to apologize for my father, but I would have none of it. When Dad tried to enter my room, I started screaming and crying hysterically. It was the kind of primitive howling a parent will promise anything to make stop, but I was inconsolable. *"Keep him away from me!!!"* I shouted. Whenever my father tried to approach the door, confusing a lull in the storm with its end or thinking that I might be experiencing a change of heart, I would start all over again.

Ironically, if I had to identify a specific event that saved my relationship with my father, that episode on the turnpike and night spent crying uncontrollably in my room might be it. That small act of defiance safeguarded a future for my father and me.

Dad's betrayal of me wasn't able to cause me to betray myself. I refused to enter into such an unholy alliance with him.

Jean-Paul Sartre was wrong when he wrote his famous existential maxim: "Hell is other people." Hell is not other people; it is our need for other people.

Like all sons, I needed my father then, and I still need him now.

The Elements

I was born of a marriage of fire and water. My father's rage and my mother's drinking needed some earth to ground them. I was that mud. My brother floated like air above them, blown and carried away on the winds of their fiery union. To this day he remains the same elusive element, impossible to hold or capture. Sorely missed when he's not there, barely noticeable when he is. But I stayed put. Roots firmly planted in the earth, I soaked up the rays from my father's bright star, hoping, praying it wouldn't scorch or singe me with its blistering heat. The moisture from my mother's tears and milk sustained and fed me, when it wasn't threatening to wash me away.

In 1970 my father took another sabbatical. This time we spent the year living in London. On school vacations we traveled to such places as Paris, Florence, and Rome—the way living in New Jersey, you might pack the kids in the car and drive to Buffalo, Philly, or Cape May.

My father was always at his worst when he traveled. I have a memory of the four of us in our Citröen station wagon speeding along at more than seventy miles per hour on France's version of the Autobahn. Mom was at the wheel. Dad, in the throes of one of his rages, grabbed my mother's hair and started hitting her. My brother and I sat huddled together in the backseat. "Malcolm, stop, have you gone mad!?!" she shouted while slamming on the brakes. We thought we were going to die.

That year, Mom started behaving oddly. It began with her hiding her journals in places my brother and I couldn't help but find them. She hid them in the closets on top of piles of sheets and towels, and when that seemed to require too much effort on her part, she would just leave them in plain view on a chair or sofa in front of the television. Just ten and fourteen years of age at the time, of course we read them.

She talked of wanting to leave my father and wrote that she was only staying with him because of us. She said she felt strangled—I remember that word showing up over and over again. Her writing sounded drunk and incoherent, a stream of consciousness, full of vulgarities, that would repeat the same phrase over and over again. She said she felt dead inside and talked about all the hypocrisies of a life lived with my father. (That's when I knew she hadn't gone completely crazy, as everything she said about what it was like to live with him was true.)

For as long as I could remember, my mother had always served as a floodgate for my father's angry torrents. That year in England and during the period leading up to my parents' divorce, after years of laboring in service of her psyche (and my brother's and mine), the levee was starting to break.

Alcohol and tears filled the streets and pathways of her life like one of those river towns on the banks of the Mississippi following a devastating rain—the houses, stores, and offices are all still there, the infrastructure, but the water renders them useless. Nothing going in, nothing going out. All activity except that which has to do with surviving or cleaning up from the flood comes to a halt.

Our mother, our safe harbor, our rock, our isle of sanity, our shelter from the storm, had become a disaster site. And all my brother and I could do was stand on the rooftops of the buildings and hope we didn't drown while waiting for help to arrive. It never did.

At least not that year.

9

Mom

All women become like their mothers. That is their
tragedy. No man does. That's his.

—OSCAR WILDE

SOMETIMES WHEN I SIT in my office listening to my client Rose
describe her love for her ten-year-old son, I feel both a yearning
and a profound sense of sadness and loneliness wash over me. It's
as if she's telling me a story about someone I once knew or something that happened to me in another life. Mostly what I experience is a kind of reverence and awe.

One morning, she shared a passage from her journal about
what had happened the night before when she went into her son's
room to tuck him in and give him his goodnight hug and kiss:

He threw his body onto mine like it was a life raft, home,
the shore. I thought of whoever it is who will end up loving him grownup to grownup and said a prayer that it's
good between them—that she will love him well, that he
will know how to love her well, that they will be life rafts

147

for each other. I hug him with that kind of love, so he will know what it feels like and know what to look for and know when he's found it.

The far-reaching impact of mothers on the souls of men is a classic theme of literature and psychology. As Bob Blauner observed in his anthology *Our Mothers' Spirits*, the larger culture as well as modern psychology instructs us to separate from our mothers—psychically as well as physically—and to identify instead with our fathers: "The idea behind 'Like father, like son' seems self-evident. Not so its cognate: 'Like mother, like son.'"

In my own case, I'm very clear that any benefit I derived from my relationship with my father was a direct result of my mother's efforts. Her imprint can be found on every important event of my life, including my father's death.

I want to resist writing about sinners and saints. Neither of my parents was either. But the fact is, like most men of his generation (and many of my own), my father didn't have a clue how to raise a son or parent a child, and was utterly dependent on my mother for guidance and direction. Compassion, patience, empathy, tenderness—these are things my mother taught my father and me (although he wasn't always the best student).

My mother's love, perseverance, and sacrifice at the beginning of my life provided me the skills and resilience needed to forge the special bond and close relationship my father and I enjoyed at the end of his.

Flying Washing Machines

When I was growing up, my mother was my best friend. It is for me one of the tragedies of my life that I was able to reap such a rewarding adult relationship with my father and connection with him at the end of his life, but when it comes to my relationship with my mother—the person who made all that possible—I'm not able to enjoy the same.

How did this happen?

I used to think it had to do with her drinking, but after talking to other men who have lost their fathers, I found that this growing distance between us was an experience not unique to my mother and me. I can't say if this is the way it is for the majority of men, but it speaks to the experience of a significant minority of men's relationships with their mothers (at least of the men I see in my practice and interviewed when researching this book). And while it manifests differently in each mother-son-father triangle, there are common themes.

As another writer observed, our culture's historical assignment of relationship work to women has turned emotions into a disregarded "second language" for men. As a consequence, mothers often take on the role of "emotional interpreter" for fathers and sons. Some sons rebel against what they perceive as their mother's constant interference. Others welcome it early on, but eventually outgrow the need for their mother's assistance. Either way, over time, as a result of these and similar kinds of interactions, we lose sight of our mothers as people in their own right, separate from the restrictive roles they're cast in.

Growing up, I had a very one-dimensional view of my mother. I'm not thinking of the typical ways in which sons see their mothers as existing to intuit and service their every want and need—although I certainly exhibited a good deal of that sort of behavior during my formative years. At least I did until my mother went to law school when she was forty-three years old and I was just thirteen, which was my first real initiation into the world of feminism and women's identity development.

I remember standing next to her as she showed me how to operate our washer-dryer unit; with its strange configuration of buttons and dials it looked like an alien spacecraft. "It's really not that complicated" is all I recall her saying after the fifteen minutes she spent explaining all the functions and purposes of the various cycles and settings. That and the merciful look on her face, half compassion, half astonishment, as if it was one of the great mysteries of life that she and I could have come from the same species, never mind the same family.

I also remember the panic following my test launch, when the bubbles just kept getting bigger and bigger and started seeping out the glass portal, soaking the carpeting and spilling into my room across the hall. I felt like Curious George in the children's story when the man with the yellow hat leaves him home alone and the little monkey tries to clean up an ink spill on the man's desk with a box of laundry soap and a garden hose. To this day I've never used the proper amount of detergent to wash a load of my clothes out of fear of repeating that debacle.

Anyway, I'm not thinking of the rites of passage that result when, after years of hearing her teenager implore her to "Get a life!" a single mother decides to actually follow his advice and go out and get one for herself. What I am thinking of is that, if men and boys often feel pressured to define themselves as "other than" in relation to women, I experienced a strong need to see my mother as "other than" my father.

Dad was angry and unpredictable, Mom was gentle and reliable; he was judgmental and shaming, she was accepting and encouraging; he was scary and abusive, she was safe and loving. As a result I ended up with a very skewed view of my parents that included an idealized picture of my mother and an overly critical (though probably more deserved) understanding of my father.

My mother was the firewall between me and my father's violence, and it cost her dearly. When I was finally able see my parents for the flawed and loving people they both were, I discovered I had a lot of stored-up anger toward my mother for myriad reasons. For not leaving my father soon enough, for not protecting us better, for protecting us too much.

A Blessing in Disguise

In my conversations with other men about their interactions with their mothers after their fathers' death, I was struck by two things. The first was the level of resentment and anger they still harbored toward their surviving parent. The second was the difference in their and their mothers' attitudes about death and dying.

The latter may result from a new kind of generation gap. After all, hospice, living wills, and end-of-life care are relatively new developments in health care. However, another generational theme surfaced in my conversations with clients and the other contributors to this book; this one is unique to sons who lost their fathers at an early or young age.

One client of mine, Paul, an only child whose father died when he was just sixteen, captured the experience of these teenage and twenty-something young men in a sentence: "After my father died I started feeling like the last unicorn."

Paul said his mother started looking at him as if he were an endangered species in need of shelter and protection: "When she looked at me she saw my father's eyes. And when she held my hand she felt his firm steady clasp. For a while, I had a hard time throwing away my fingernail cuttings or discarding an eyelash for fear I was destroying a rare object and depriving my mother of something that she might want to touch or hold on to."

Being in grief is somewhat like being in love, writes the poet Mark Doty, as in both states, the imagination is entirely preoccupied with one person. In Paul's case, he and his mother found themselves obsessed with the same person, which was one aspect of the whole devastating experience that only the two of them shared.

When I asked Paul how he felt about these exchanges with his mother, he said:

At first it made me uncomfortable. But once I realized I didn't have to do anything about it, that I didn't have to take care of her or protect her either by trying to cover up the things about me that reminded her of my father, or by trying to be more like him, I wasn't bothered by it anymore. In fact, now I like when she says something I do reminds her of my father or when she sees him in me. It's comforting. I like thinking that he's not lost to us and that I carry so much of him and who he was inside of me. It's like he's with me all the time now.

I spoke to a number of men about the relation between their fathers' deaths and the nature of the resentments they carry toward their mothers. The responses I unearthed appeared complex, but perhaps they're not so hard to comprehend.

When Nick talked about his anger at his father for dying, he said, "I'm still mad at him for being gone." But then he added, "I think that's because that's what was familiar to me, Dad not being around. Him still being at the drinking club and not home. He was never there." For many men, death is the ultimate reminder of what has always been the case: Mom was there, Dad was not.

Of course, I'm speaking in generalities. The father of an adult client of mine died recently. This same client lost his mother in a tragic car accident when he was very young. After his mother's death, his father quit his job and stayed home full time to take care of the children. However, his mother's absence was such a powerful presence in their household when he was growing up that some of the same patterns we're discussing—his father's distancing and emotional unavailability and the memory of his mother's nurturing touch—were still apparent to him many years later.

Nick's effort at arriving at a more "conscious" attitude toward his mother—one not driven by unconscious conflicts, repressed longings, and old wounds—was a theme that appeared in many men's narratives. Reconceiving his relationship to his mother and his mother's life—to see her in what the psychologist Paul Olson calls her "infinite complexity," as a human being with strengths and weaknesses, rather than all good or all bad—is important work for a man. Without such a consciousness, men tend to blame their mothers for everything wrong in their lives and often will transfer such feelings to all women.

Sam (the client of mine who brought a copy of Simon Wiesenthal's *The Sunflower* to therapy) shared a fantasy he used to entertain about his father and him. Sam had an image of the two of them sitting together on the porch of their farm in Vermont where Sam and his Dad had enjoyed some of their best times together. His father would tell Sam his stories so Sam could commit them to memory, while Sam showed his father pictures of his grandchildren.

Then they would watch the sun go down and listen to the crickets chirp until his father nodded off to sleep. Of course, that's not what happened:

> I thought we had all this time. I knew he hadn't taken very good care of himself and that he'd had a lot of medical problems; still, I thought he would live forever. And then, suddenly, instead of taking care of my father the way I planned, I ended up spending the next couple of years trying to get to know my mother. We had never had an interaction that wasn't about Dad. I didn't have a clue about who she was, what she wanted from life, her hopes and dreams. We had to start from scratch.

As we know from our previous discussion of Sam, it turns out he had a lot of what the therapy community calls unresolved anger toward his father.

Initially, Sam's mother, Nancy, had difficulty with her son's grief. She missed her husband terribly. He was her best friend. She thought her son was just continuing all the senseless arguing with his father. She felt she needed to defend her husband, especially now that he was no longer there to defend himself.

More than anything, she was tired of feeling caught in the middle. She just wanted to remember the good times they had had as a family and move on. She resented her son for continuing to find fault with his father and for what Nancy perceived as Sam's constant need to relive the past.

Sam remembers his mother saying things to him that were intended to make him feel better. "Your pain will fade and you will be left with beautiful memories."

Sam understood that his mother was only trying to comfort him, but her words did not fit with his experience. "I know she means well, but my memories of my father are also about pain and turmoil, and when he died that history was just as vivid," Sam said during one of our sessions.

The process Sam was undergoing was an important, if conflicted, one. Sam loved his dad, and his father's death made him more aware of that fact than at any other time in his life. However, many of his memories of his father were unpleasant. Sam needed to find ways of honoring those as well or it was going to be increasingly difficult for him to show up for the more tender, caring experiences the two men shared.

Sam spoke about the arduous yet rewarding process his mother and he underwent witnessing each other's grief. He said it was one of the only good things that resulted from his father's death. As a result, Sam and his mother gained a newfound respect for each other as people. Sam invited Nancy to join us for several of our therapy sessions.

Before our meetings, when describing his relationship with his mother, Sam said, "We are like strangers who know each other very well." Afterward, he referred to his father's dying before his mother as "a blessing in disguise."

How can mothers and sons find ways to reach across the divide and speak about the sort of loss and trauma caused by the death of a father? And when these relationships fall apart, how can we as a culture situate ourselves and bear witness to people's hurt without having to assign fault or cast blame? Finally, how do we find ways of honoring both the connections sons feel to their fathers and the failure and pain caused by these relationships?

There are no easy answers to these questions, but I feel there are practices that can guide us as we search for resolution.

(W)rites of Passage

One of Sam's biggest regrets was that his father died alone: "There was no one at his side when he died. No one to comfort him or ease his fears about death." Sam said he wanted to be there to help his father make things right with God and, what was more important, for his father and him to make peace with each other.

In Catholicism this is what might be called giving someone his or her last rites, in which a priest offers a prayer to ease a dying person's passing and journey into the next life. In Judaism there is nothing quite equivalent, but there are two practices that come close. One is called the annulment of vows, which because of my background is a suitable alternative for me. Others can look to their particular religion or spiritual traditions for something similar.

Normally something carried out during the High Holy Days, this spiritual practice can be performed anytime during the year. As Rabbi David Cooper observes in his *God Is a Verb*, the annulment of vows basically involves confessing our regrets to another person or listening to someone else's confessions, particularly someone who is in the process of dying. By releasing our fathers from concerns about unfinished business, we can provide them with a priceless gift: liberation.

Mostly what this exercise requires is simply listening to the dying person's concerns. After they've expressed what's weighing on them, Rabbi Cooper suggests you then use appeals to reason, emotion, and your relationship with them, and if necessary, offer to bring in other people to ease their guilt or shame and help the dying person find forgiveness.

The success of this practice is not measured by the amount or intensity of information divulged or wrongs that are righted. Rather, success is measured by the degree to which a safe haven or sanctuary is provided in which a person can choose to discuss his or her regrets.

Of course, Sam wasn't able to practice any of this with his father. However, I reminded him of another Jewish ritual called *tashlich* (sending away), which is usually done annually on the afternoon of the first day of Rosh Hashanah (Jewish New Year). People say prayers at a body of water. It can be a stream, a pond, a river, a lake, or an ocean. Standing beside the water, they cast into it bread crumbs representing traits, habits, or memories they would like to discard. This exercise can be done with a dying parent in a hospital in the form of a letter or scraps of paper that can be burned afterward or destroyed in some other symbolic way. Concerns you might ask your father or the dying person to write about (or write for them if they're not able to) include: things I have done in my life that I regret, things I've said to harm someone, events I would replay if I could, things I wish I had said to someone, promises made that were never kept, hopes and dreams that never worked out.

The timing of such a ritual is something people often ask about. When is it appropriate to introduce such a conversation and how should it be done? Should a son wait until his father mentions his regrets?

The short answer is that there is no right or wrong way to go about this. If you bring it up, your father will let you know if he's uncomfortable with the idea. If he can no longer speak, he will indicate his discomfort with his body language. Even so, there are ways for a son to have this conversation without his father's participation.

I told Sam I saw no reason this couldn't be done by a son after his father's death, no matter how long ago he died. In Sam's case I suggested he modify his concerns in the following way: things I said to my father I regret, things I wish I had said to my father, events I would replay between us if I could, my prayer for my father.

After Sam completed this ritual, he and his mother took the scraps of paper to a lake near their farm house in Vermont. Nancy read a poem by Raymond Carver, one of her husband's favorite writers, and then Sam tore up his prayers and regrets and sent them away. Here is the poem Nancy read:

LATE FRAGMENT
And did you get what
you wanted from this life, even so?
I did.
And what did you want?
To call myself beloved, to feel myself
beloved on this earth.

My Ritual

The period from November 6, my father's birthday, to December 27, his memorial day, is the hardest time of year for me. Some years it stretches to the anniversary of his memorial service, which took place on February 8. I was, until my father's death, indifferent to the holidays, but now they're pretty tough.

On the first night of Hanukkah, a few weeks shy of the first anniversary of my father's death, I received a phone call. When I picked up the receiver, it was my mother's voice on the other end of the phone.

"I know you had a routine of calling your father so you could light the candles together," she said, sounding a little awkward. "I realize it wouldn't be quite the same and I understand if you'd rather not. . . . But I thought that maybe you might like to light them with me. I could call you later this evening if you like . . ." She was calling from her home in California. I remember the phone kept crackling static. But even though our connection wasn't a good one, her message came through loud and clear.

"I like that idea, Mom. I like it a lot. It would mean a great deal to me. Why don't you call us around six tonight," I replied, and I hurried to hang up the phone. I didn't want my mother to hear me cry.

That single act was one of the most loving things my mother has ever done for me, and that's saying a lot. It communicated so much. First and foremost, she alone understood how hard this was for me. While she couldn't replace my father, hearing my mother's voice on the other end of the line and singing the songs and prayers with her helped me make it through the evening. We repeated this ritual for the next seven nights. And now both my sons call every Hanukkah to sing the prayers to her.

Had that been all my mother accomplished with that phone call, it would have been enough. But it was more than that. She helped me make peace with my parents' tumultuous marriage. My mother's gesture wasn't just about consolation, it was about reconciliation.

———

The Portrait

In his study, books, books, and books kept filling up the boxes I placed in front of the shelves that had been their home for ten, twenty, thirty, forty years—in some cases, more than a half a century. These were his closest companions, his intimates and beloveds—the ones that had survived more than a dozen office moves and changes of residence, when many other titles had been sold off to used book stores and rare book collectors, or given away to library drives.

It was a literary funeral procession in my father's honor. Dad had marked the pages of his texts with thin paper bookmarks, hundreds of them, made from the torn pages of discarded lecture notes, pen scribbles across them like some ancient Sanskrit. On this day they waved from the jacket covers and bindings like banners of the lost tribes of Israel.

Now that they had outlasted him, what was to become of them? Where were they going? Who was going to look after them? Would families be broken up? What about the foreign language titles—who would understand them? How would anyone know what they were saying? I told the Hebrew ones I planned on learning how to speak and read their language so I could pass it on to my sons. "You will be treated better than your editors and publishers treated my people," I sniped at the German titles.

What started out as a labor of love soon became a frenzied effort to get the job done. Plans for thoughtful conversations

with my stepmother about whether she wanted to read a particular title or hold on to it as a keepsake evolved into a race
against the clock to get as many books into the empty boxes
with as little discussion as possible.

It was horrifying. Wittgenstein's *Tractatus Logico-
Philosophicus* stacked on top of *Portnoy's Complaint*, weathered
hard covers of Buber's *I and Thou* and *Tales of the Hassidim*
wedged up against the smooth, shiny surface of Erica Jong's
Fear of Flying, all packed in boxes marked "California Oranges"
or "Dole Bananas" some with the Styrofoam packaging still
inside.

In the basement I found some photographs in an old tattered box along with some memorabilia from his college days.
One was a class photograph from Dad's yeshiva. He must have
been just nine or ten years old at the time. I had no trouble picking him out. It was his smile. His pensive look, his eyes.

I spread them out on the floor and pored over them with a
fascination that bordered on mania. I couldn't stop looking at
them. They were sacred relics. I wanted them to tell me things I
hadn't known before, reveal some hidden truth. I studied each
one intensely, absorbing every facet, the detailed carvings on the
border of the paper mat that the school photographs had been
sent home in. Every shadow, every swath of light. As Paul Auster
writes in his *Invention of Solitude*, "I wanted the images to
become a part of me. I wanted nothing to be lost."

In his bedroom closest, stashed away in the back behind his
suits—he may have even forgotten it was there—I found a large
painted portrait of my father that I'd never seen before. I recognized the artist immediately as his best friend Jack Blumenthal,
whose death fifteen years earlier had left a huge hole in my
father's life.

The portrait was a gigantic five feet by five feet and hideous.
It looked as if it had been painted in the early seventies. The
colors were loud and gaudy, the brush strokes large, bold, and

undisciplined. I got the sense that just having it inside the house, even storing it in the back of his closet, was a compromise Dad might have had some difficulty hammering out with his wife, Denise. They had both a basement and a garage, after all. But as garish as it was, it had a certain aura or light that captured my father's spirit. Even Denise acknowledged that much. I loved it. The negotiations were not difficult. "Please," said Denise, "do you have room for it this trip?"

I took the painting to a framer whom I'd arranged ahead of time to bring the photographs to, so they could be ready for Dad's memorial service. I've never seen the English language get such a workout as when the shopkeeper and her assistant tried to come up with the right words to describe this offering laid out before them.

When finished, it was a miracle! The corners were repaired and the chips on the canvas touched up. It glowed from the inside out. Its transformation complete, and to my wife's shock and horror, I hung it up in our dining room (where it remains today). When I carried it into the house, I asked my son Julian, just ten months at the time, "Who's that a picture of?" "Grand-pops!" he exclaimed. "That's right," I answered, and I started to cry.

PART THREE

SAYING GOOD-BYE

Ever has it been that love knows not its own depth until the hour of separation.

—KAHLIL GIBRAN, *THE PROPHET*

10

"Is This What I Want to Do with My Death?"

Teaching Our Sons about Death and Dying

How do we learn to die? Most of us spend our lives avoiding that question. In her *Intimate Death: How the Dying Teach Us How to Live*, the psychologist Marie de Hennezel wrote, "We hide death as if it were shameful and dirty. We see in it only horror, meaninglessness, useless struggle and suffering, an intolerable scandal, whereas it is our life's culmination, its crowning moment, and what gives it both sense and worth."

We live in a death-denying culture. As another expert on death and bereavement practices said:

> In Western society we relegate death to the back rooms, to the parts of the nursing homes and hospitals where people don't go. When we do see death on TV or video games or at the movies, it is really "pretend death." We've gotten to the point where most people will live a significant part of their lives without ever seeing a dead person, and fewer still will ever touch someone who is dead. When a relative dies in a nursing home or a hospital, the first thing many people want to do is to call someone and have the body

taken away. I believe this is a conditioned response in our society. It is not necessarily a natural response.

This fear of the dying has created a gap in our ability to mourn and heal when faced with death. Men perhaps more than any other segment of the population in post-industrial society have suffered from the breakup of religious institutions and community rituals that people traditionally looked to for guidance and solace when grieving.

The final section of this book teaches us how to turn death from something lonely and agonizing into something sacred. Demonstrated are the importance of an honest reckoning, the value of ritual, and the necessity of touch.

Part of every father's job is to teach his son about death. The lesson doesn't have to be Talmudic, but there has to be some kind of learning passed on that will be useful. It can be dramatic, such as the courage Nick's dad showed when he turned down a potentially lifesaving operation and turned to face death instead. Or it can be as simple as the peace that came at the end of a life of hard work lived with decency and integrity as passed on to Lenny by his father Stan.

And, as is often the case with fathers, the most important lessons are the ones they teach us at those odd moments when they aren't trying to teach us at all.

The Wedding Photograph

In Watertown the weather was gorgeous. Spring had arrived. The trees on the surrounding hills cast a warm red glow from the buds on the maples readying to open. Everywhere you look this time of year, you see and smell possibility. With rebirth all around, it's a tough time of year to say good-bye to those who have died.

At the funeral home, Nick and his sister Pam were busily putting pictures of Crash on the tables around the room where his father's viewing was to be held. They both had brought some of their own photos and borrowed a few from his father's girl-friend. Nick thought it would be a nice way of evoking Crash's spirit and helping others to remember him the way their family did. However, before Nick could undertake arranging his father's childhood photographs, there was the minor detail of seeing his father's body.

When he was just a small child, Nick had seen his nine-year-old cousin in a coffin, who of course was just a child himself. He's had a fear of people lying in coffins ever since. And this time it was his father, which was the most dreadful thing he could imagine.

Nick stood on the porch of the funeral home contemplating his dilemma. His first thought was of a more existential or philo-sophical nature: "Stupid, fucking open casket people!" he said to his sister. His second, third, and fourth were more immediate ones about what he was going to encounter inside: "If I open the door, am I going to see him or do we have to go through a hall first? And will I be able to retreat when I see his body?"

Those were just a few of his thoughts as he turned the door handle and entered the building. Luckily, mercifully, there was a foyer. Nick eased his way into the entranceway with its high ceil-ings, walked around a corner, and there it was—his father's body laid out in the casket, resting peacefully in a sea of red satin. "It wasn't as bad as I thought it was going to be, but it was pretty awful," recalled Nick.

Oddly, while Nick was expecting to be overwhelmed by the sight of his father's body, it was its size that shocked him most. Nick doesn't remember when his father had become so over-weight and out of shape, but there was no denying it. He took one look at his father and said to himself, "I never want to look like that." Nick was so consumed by his thoughts, he didn't notice there was someone standing next to him, but now the man was speaking to him. It was the funeral director. It took a minute for his words to register: "Your father's size made things very difficult, he was so big," he said. "God, how did he let himself get so big?" Nick didn't know how to respond. What gave this man, almost a complete stranger, the impression it was okay to say such things about his father, and why was he saying them to him?

The funeral director's remarks angered Nick—especially the polite tone in his voice—but he also felt intense shame. Suddenly, Nick's shoes felt too large and the sleeves of his jacket too long, like when he was a child playing dress-up with his parents' clothes. And he wasn't standing next to Crash's open casket, he was in his house in Watertown, a nine-year-old boy waiting for his father to come home from work.

Nick heard the T-bird's tires scream—"Dad's home!"—the way they always did when his father turned into the driveway. Nick heard his father's car door slam, and instead of waiting for his son to run out to greet him like he always did, Crash rushed into the house and went straight to the bathroom. Nick stood in the hallway waiting for his father to come out. When he finally did, Nick could tell that his father had just brushed his teeth and washed his face. He was still combing his hair when he passed Nick in the hallway. His dad flew by him en route to the kitchen to make himself a cup of coffee. But before descending the stairs, Crash reached clumsily for Nick and, using his son's head to steady himself, tousled Nick's hair.

A little while later, the police came to the house and wanted to talk to his father. He took them out on the porch. Nick listened from the window. His father had been involved in a hit-and-run accident. He hadn't hurt anybody. He just had wrecked somebody's car—smashed into it and drove off. It was the first time Nick became aware of how totally compromised his father's integrity was as a result of his drinking. It was also the first time Nick remembers that his father—who brought home the best presents, drove the coolest cars, and took care of people in the community—seemed ugly to him.

When Nick snapped back to the present, the funeral director was gone. He had only himself to confess to, that what bothered him most about this man's remarks was that he knew just what he meant. Nick was both heartbroken and repulsed by his father's appearance, just as he had been all those years ago. It was a painful feeling, but it was one he was used to. He'd spent most of his adult life declaring that he didn't want to be like his father. He didn't want to drink like him and he didn't want to act like him. Seeing his father's body and hearing the funeral director's words brought on a wave of guilt. And fear.

Nick keeps his copy of his parents' wedding photograph on his dresser at home. He greets his father's twenty-something dapper image every morning when he rises and every night before he goes to bed. Nick has never thought he looked like his dad. And when he looks at that photograph he realizes he is right, he doesn't look *like* his father. He looks *exactly* like him. "I can see that now, and it scares me to death," he said. Seeing his dad lying there lifeless, all of a sudden the understanding that he too was going to die someday became more real to Nick. "Knowing that reality," he said, "has been, depending on the day, either scary as shit or a reminder of the preciousness of time and family and doing what you like for work."

Special Delivery

In Rochester winter receives its last rites later than most other cities. Every March people eagerly perform the long deathwatch, hoping the end will be swift and painless. For men like Lenny and Stan (the computer programmer and the stonemason) this dreadful waiting means only one thing: spring training! The beginning of an eight-week period marked by snowmelt, long shadows, false hopes, and endless talk of baseball. Sometimes they would drive down to Florida to see the Red Sox and the other boys of summer polish their skills and remove the rust from their games. Lenny's dad used to say, "God invented spring training so men don't have to wait until July to taste ballpark franks."

But this winter neither Lenny nor Stan had a clue how their bull pens were shaping up or how many of their favorite players would be sold, cut, traded, or otherwise missing when their teams regrouped in Boston and Cincinnati in April. This season Lenny would know more about Merkel cell than he would about any of his Major League heroes who had ever played the game.

In fact, today was the day word came back that the cancer was in his father's spine. This was it; there was nothing more the doctors could do for him. When Lenny heard this news, he left Rochester and drove six hours through the night to pick up his wife and children from their home in western Massachusetts, only to shower, eat, turn the car around, and drive them all straight back to Rochester.

"I brought you a special delivery," Lenny said to his father. Charlie and Henry walked into their grandfather's room wearing expressions of fear wrapped in curiosity. They hadn't seen their grandfather in a while and they had a kid's idea of someone dying; they didn't really know what to expect. What they saw was their grandfather lying in a bed hooked up to all kinds of machines. Then they heard their grandfather's voice.

"How much does Grandpa love you?" he asked. Both children broke into smiles. "Soooo much!" they answered in unison, and ran up to him so they could wrap their arms around him.

Lenny's father had been in and out of consciousness all day, but he was present for that moment. Then Stan, holding his "overnight packages" in both arms, looked up at his son, whose eyes were filling with tears, and said, "You can bury me now, I'm ready to go."

Lenny never forgot the sight of his father sitting up in his hospital bed connected to all those wires and tubes, his arms wrapped around both grandchildren. Throughout his life, Stan had made one sacrifice after another for his family. Lenny often wondered whether his father felt it was worth it, but he never had the nerve to ask him. The truth is, he wasn't sure he wanted to hear his reply. In the end, with his family gathered around him, his father's answer was clear.

Atonement

When it comes to the subject of atonement, Ervin and his estranged father, Albert, represent a powerful example of reconciliation and forgiveness.

As Albert neared the end of his battle with cancer, Ervin arranged to take the spring semester off from school in order to spend time with his dad and to help his relatives care for him.

Shortly after moving into his father's home in Georgia, Ervin asked his father if there was anything he wanted to accomplish in the next few months that Ervin could help him with. Ervin was thinking along the lines of correspondence, phone calls, or a household project like putting all his father's photographs and cards in an album. Albert said there was one thing, and proceeded to ask his son the one thing Ervin didn't think he could pull off. His father wanted to arrange a visit with his ex-wife, Ervin's mother, so Albert could see her one last time before he died.

The only way Ervin's mother, Dorothy, had agreed to let him go to Georgia was if he promised to check in with her by phone at least twice a week. Ervin promised. But in fact, he found himself speaking to his mother on an almost daily basis. Helping his father die was more difficult than anything Ervin had ever done in his life or could ever imagine himself doing. His nightly phone calls with his mother were a source of great comfort, but Ervin never asked her if she wanted to speak to his dad.

So when his father asked his son's help, Ervin decided to write his mother a letter instead of broaching the subject on the phone. After receiving her son's letter, Dorothy told Ervin that she had already considered a visit, and while she believed it was a good idea, she needed to give it some more thought before making a decision one way or the other. Ervin said she shouldn't wait too long to make up her mind, as his father was now in hospice. A few days later, during one of their nightly check-ins, Dorothy said she had arranged to take a Friday and a Monday off from work and would be there in two weeks.

In the days leading up to his mother's visit, Ervin's father's condition worsened significantly. New devices seemed to be arriving daily at the house, crowding out the number of people his father's tiny room could hold. There was a hospital bed, oxygen tanks, and a machine that dispensed pain medication through an IV drip that his father could control, which, Ervin noticed, appeared to be running constantly.

Ervin picked his mother up at Savannah's airport. They mostly made small talk on their way back to his father's house. Stepping into Albert's bedroom, Dorothy was shocked and unprepared for the sight of her ex-husband's emaciated, diseased body. Albert opened his eyes and slowly focused on her.

"You came," he said, holding out one of his hands.

"I did," said Dorothy, taking his hand in hers.

"I don't know what I'd have done without this young man here," his father said, pointing to Ervin.

"He's a good guy," his mother replied flatly.

There was an awkward silence.

"Can I get you anything, Pops?" asked Ervin.

"I'm okay, son," his dad answered. "He's always looking out for me," said his father to his mother.

"I see that," said Dorothy with a little more warmth in her voice.

Ervin watched his father's eyes fill up with his mother. And for the first time in his life, Ervin understood how the two of them had ended up together.

"He gets that from you," continued Albert. "Always taking care of people. Always knowing what to do and just how to do it . . . you were always the strong one . . ."

"Please don't," interrupted Dorothy; but Albert pressed on.

"I'm sorry I didn't take more responsibility. . . . I'm sorry I wasn't a better husband to you and father to Ervin when I had a chance. I'm sorry for . . ." Ervin felt a large salty tear trickle down his cheek and into his mouth. He noticed a puddle of tears starting to form on his dad's cheek as well. Ervin grabbed a damp washcloth from his father's bedside table, wiped his own tears with his shirtsleeve, and used the washcloth to dab his father's face. "I'm sorry for how I treated you, Dorothy. You deserved better," Albert continued. "And I know . . . you don't owe me a thing and I'm not asking you for anything . . . I don't deserve . . . "

"I forgive you, Albert," said his mother, interrupting his father again. "I'm sorry you're so sick and that you won't get to spend more time with your son."

Albert started to weep, and now Dorothy was crying, too. She was still holding Albert's hand. Albert reached for his son and squeezed Ervin's hand tightly, and for the next twenty minutes, the three of them just sat together, talking, crying, and passing tissues back and forth.

At the onset of his illness, every terminal patient harbors hope of a miraculous recovery. However, as death approaches, his prayers (and ours) become more modest in scope. The desire to witness the birth of a grandchild, a daughter's wedding, or a son's graduation may be all that's left to maintain not only the optimism but the life of a dying person. Sometimes a dying man's source of hope can be as undemanding as the wish to say "thank you," "forgive me," or "I love you," to someone important or even someone they didn't know that well but whose presence in their life held particular meaning.

Ervin's mother stayed another couple of days. The morning after she left, Ervin's father slipped into a coma. He died the following day.

Before his father died, Ervin said he felt as if his life was a script. Everything seemed as if it were already mapped out in front of him. He felt that if he diverged even a little from what was expected of him, he would be letting everyone down. But watching his father die, he realized there are things worse than dying; like being alive but feeling dead inside.

This whole death experience—event, episode, living hell?—whatever you want to call it with my father is the most alive I've ever felt in my life. True, parts of it were agonizing, but I was so totally present. Nothing comes close to it. I've experienced moments like it on the court—a state of grace—but that was just a forty-minute game. This was twenty-four/seven. Everything seemed so vivid and clear.

I understand that a lot of what I'm feeling has to do with missing my dad and my trying to hold on to something precious he and I got to share. I don't want to lose this feeling of being so awake. Now that I've experienced it, I don't want to go back. I don't want to be one of those people who moves through life like one of the walking dead.

I know the feeling Ervin spoke of. There is an experience of aliveness that only seems available to us when we're in the presence of death. It is a very compelling, almost spiritual experience. But Ervin underwent another experience at his father's deathbed that I recognized. This one was more about shedding feelings than accessing them, and the psychological and emotional weight lifted from Ervin shoulders as a result was almost palpable.

When a father abandons or traumatizes his son, he is in a state of shamelessness. The shame he does not consciously feel will be absorbed, along with other unconscious feelings, by his son. The author Pia Melody called these transmitted states "carried shame" and "carried feeling." They are the means by which the wound and legacy of pain are passed from father to son across generations. Carried feeling and carried shame are, according to the therapist Terry Real, the psychological seeds of depression, which can lead to our moving through life feeling the way Ervin describes it, like one of the "walking dead."

When Albert made his amends to Dorothy, he took back some of the shame his son had been carrying for him all those years, and in so doing taught his son another important lesson about dying. While we can't undo the past, what a man chooses to do with his death can have as profound impact on the world and the people around him as the choices he makes in life.

My Lesson

"I'm sixty-six," my father used to boast, "and my only medical problem is a trick knee that interferes with running, skiing, and tennis." So on a beautiful spring morning, with no sense of foreboding, he entered his doctor's office and settled into a chair.

"You have multiple myeloma," my father's doctor said. "It's a form of cancer. We'll have to do a biopsy to confirm it, but the tests are conclusive."

Those were the words that swung my father into his new life. He had walked into his doctor's office full of life and vitality. Death had been a neurotic tune he talked about in his lectures, an existential theme park he took his students to where they could enjoy the scares and thrills of rides on Nietzsche, Heidegger, Kierkegaard, and others. Now suddenly it was his destination; he sat there numb.

It was March 29, 1991, and that night was the Passover Seder. Dad sang robustly, but with a sense that it was for the last time.

In 1991 I was working at a hospital in the Berkshires. My father called me at work to tell me the news. "Are you going to be okay, Dad?" I asked. He tried to play down the seriousness of what he was saying. "I don't mind having a terminal illness, so long as it doesn't interfere with my health," he joked. I wasn't buying it.

When I hung up the phone, I immediately called the hospital's oncology department. I spoke to the head nurse and asked her about my father's condition. I told her that I did not want her to sugarcoat her remarks. "I need facts and information. I need to know what I'm dealing with. I counsel people around end-of-life issues. You can level with me," I assured her. "His plasma cells are reproducing at a great rate and not dying. They're clogging the bone marrow and interfering with the production of his white and red blood cells. Your father has a year to live, maybe two," she said somberly.

I wanted to kill her.

Back in Princeton, my father was receiving the same sort of upbeat news from his doctors. Consultations plunged him into major hospital centers—my father called them the maze of Kafka's Castle. You check in and get your number and everywhere you're treated with excessive kindness that lets you know you're in trouble. In one center, the solicitude was so overwhelming, my father told the consultant it brought to mind the line from Dante's *Inferno*: "Abandon all hope, you who enter here." To his credit, the doctor laughed.

This specialist was typical of the cancer doyens my father encountered: they are dedicated and knowledgeable, but not omniscient. My father wasn't dead within the year or even two; in fact, he lived for almost another seven years.

In the end, I wasn't angry with my colleague for the abbreviated timeline she had given my father. I was grateful. It was because of his cancer diagnosis that we were able to find each other again. As a result, when the end finally came, Dad and I had few regrets. What's more, we had such a good time en route to that moment.

It seems very strange to think one could enjoy his father's dying. Stranger still, my father seemed to be enjoying it even more than I was. We used to laugh about it. Dad said he wouldn't object to dying, if it weren't followed by death. We knew it was absurd, but what could we do?

As with my client Ervin's father, Dad's life was testament to the fact that even as he is dying, a father can accomplish meaningful tasks and grow in ways that are important to his son and family. And, lest we forget, the process of dying is no easy task; sometimes it is an accomplishment in and of itself.

His Last Hours

When I entered my father's room in ICU and heard the beeping and squawking of monitors, the hissing of respirators and pistoned mattresses, the flashing multicolored electronic signals—the whole of what Sherwin Nuland calls the "technological panoply" of modern medicine—I didn't feel like a witness to my father's death, I felt like a witness to his murder. However, it wasn't my father's body or soul that was being killed; it was his hope of having the kind of death he wanted.

Dad's treatment during his last twenty-four hours was based not on his goals but on his doctor's goals and on the accepted code of his specialty. Dad's oncologist pursued a form of futility that deprived my father of his wish to leave this world without interference where an opportunity arose.

Against the pleadings of his wife and the voice of his living will, which remains our loved ones' most reliable and verifiable way of speaking to us from the dead, my father's doctor wasn't able to let him go of his own accord. Instead, my father suffered the fate of so many of today's hospitalized dying, which is to be separated from the world by the very biotechnology and professional standards that are meant to return people to a meaningful life.

In his *How We Die*, the author and physician Sherwin Nuland writes, "In the name of Hippocrates, doctors have invented the most exquisite form of torture ever known to man: survival." My father wasn't interested in surviving. He had lived a full-impact life. In his case, the word "lived" is a misnomer. He consumed life. Devoured it. And he had the same outlook toward his health.

After he was diagnosed, for six, almost seven years Dad would be bedridden by a virus one day and go out running the next, as if he were acting out a private joke of health and youth, the joke of endlessness.

So when I arrived at the hospital and saw my father, the first thing I did was call Dad's longtime physician. "How did this happen?" I asked him. "I knew your father," he answered. "Your dad had an incredible will to live. We'd faced this sort of crisis many times over the course of his illness, and I know that if there was even the slightest possibility of his pulling out of this, if there was any chance of his getting another two or three months of life, he would have wanted me to do everything in my power to help him. I couldn't take away his only hope."

"I couldn't take away his only hope." I repeated the words to myself, but not to his physician. How do you communicate to a well-meaning doctor trying to save your father's life that hope can still exist even when rescue is impossible?

In my father's case, the situation was complicated by the strong bond he shared with his physician. After hearing what had happened, one of my father's old nurses from oncology told me that my father's doctor had a reputation for holding on to his patients for too long. "He needs to learn how to let go," she said compassionately.

In retrospect, many of the most cherished times I spent with my father were the result of this doctor's skill and dedication.

Nonetheless, when I hung up, I was furious with the doctor. His description of how it would look much worse than it was when we removed Dad's breathing tube the next day, as we agreed we would do if he didn't die in the night, did not help. "It's only a reflex, he won't suffer," he tried to reassure me. My upset with the doctor was a familiar feeling, one I'd experienced for years with my father. I wanted to tell him off, but I didn't want to alienate him. It was a needy kind of anger. The sort that asks, "Can you risk it? Can you afford to lose me?"

His Body

I experienced a remarkable serenity in the final hours I spent with my father before he died. Sitting at his bedside in ICU, death all around us, just him and me. No anger. No arguing. No tension. No disappointment. All the conflict just dissolved away. It was the most peaceful, unencumbered time I've ever felt in his presence. There was no "him" or "me" any longer, just a quiet, still "us."

I didn't want to let go. I don't mean of him; he was already gone. He had been for some time. No more fighting or resisting. His body decayed and cancer-ridden, all that was left of him was his presence (his spirit, if you prefer). I didn't want to let go of the feeling I experienced at his deathbed. I didn't want to leave the comfort of being with him in this way.

People do not disappear when they die. The closest thing I can liken it to is holding a baby immediately after its birth. When my sons Julian and Oliver were born, their gazes were so piercing and intimate, more than anything I'd ever experienced. They could look into your eyes for hours, which felt like days, on end without looking away. It was intense. No inhibitions. None whatsoever.

It was the same with Dad. Except with him, the process happened more gradually. All the trappings of life—the neuroses, the vanity, his temper tantrums—slowly over time he was stripped of them all, including his modesty. By the end, he had few bodily functions left that were his own. Not much to be vain about at that point. His job was to breathe and just be.

Eventually, when his organs finally gave out and he was declared "officially dead" by the overzealous doctor and no longer "just resting"—to borrow a line from one of his favorite Monty Python numbers—his spirit didn't fade to black with the rest of him. In fact, it came back stronger than ever.

Death transfigured Dad in minutes, and I saw the beauty of his younger days reassert itself on his blurred, careworn face. It was like something in music, the reestablishing of the original key in one of the hundreds of symphonies he used to conduct in his living room or the resolution with which he would return to the main theme in one of his lectures on Buber, Niebuhr, or Wittgenstein.

After my father died, he seemed more present, not less so. Sitting with my father that way, and then having to leave his room so they could "move him downstairs"—which is a euphemism for placing his body on a hard cold slab in a refrigerated room—gave me a visceral sense of the purpose that wakes serve. The intense desire to feel, see, and touch the body. Not just to take in the reality of his death, but also to spend more time with the person, to be in his presence a little longer. Because you know that everyday life, with all its petty demands and the huge expenditure of energy it takes to meet them, is going to swoop in any minute and make it that much harder, if not impossible, to get back to that place.

Eventually a memorial day or birthday comes and goes without being remembered. You might not realize that you forgot it until several days later. The realization is disconcerting. It's like completely forgetting or almost missing one's own wedding anniversary. Except there's no one there to chastise you or make you feel guilty, which, after all, would be better than nothing and a kind of remembering, if not a form of remembrance.

And if you do confess to others your terrible conduct, they don't say, "That's awful! What are you going to do to make up for your disrespect?" No, it's just the opposite—they commend you: "That's great! This must mean that you're finally letting go of him and moving on." But we don't want to celebrate. We want to cry. It's like losing him all over again; first the man, then our memory of him.

Death ends a life, not a relationship.

Learning to accept and even welcome the endings in our lives is the most important lesson a father can teach his son about death and dying. The grace with which Stan faced his death was something that Lenny spoke about at his father's funeral:

> Dad told his doctors that he didn't want to be attached to machines when he died. He said he wanted to die as himself—"with my head held high"—so that when he faced death the people who loved him would still find him recognizable. It was the hope that he would be Stan to his last breath, and that he would be remembered for the way he lived.

The following day a doctor came in to oversee the removal of all the equipment. When the last IV was detached from his father's wrist and a nurse wheeled the monitors and other machines away from his bed, his father, grinning from ear to ear, raised both arms out to his sides—the sleeves of his hospital gown hanging off them like bird wings—and proclaimed: "Ah, free!"

I didn't have to work hard to find the lessons buried in my father's death. They were in an article he wrote on coping with cancer. One he emphasized over and over is that we don't have to wait for a doctor to tell us that we have twelve months to live to spend more time with the people we love or to do the things that bring us joy. Unfortunately, many sons don't learn this lesson until they find out their fathers are dying; but that, they soon discover, is not necessarily a terrible thing.

Being chosen to accompany and care for a dying person as their witness is an honor. While it isn't possible for every son to be at his father's side when the man dies, when it does happen, it's a gift. These are just some of the lessons that Crash, Stan, Albert, and Mal gifted their sons with.

When discussing his father's death seven years prior, Nick said:

> For years the memories were almost too painful to bear. The images were familiar ones. I'd seen them in movies and read about them in books. The scene where the grief-stricken son throws himself on the coffin, or a teenager drops flowers into her father's grave; it's all very sentimental. But the thing is, when it's *your* father's funeral and not some character in a book or person in a movie, everything changes. When it's your father's death, it's simply unbearable.

For many sons, learning to accept death is something our fathers taught us; learning how to let go of our fathers is a lesson we learn from God.

———

The Apparition

After five days spent writing around the clock, I needed some exercise. I promised my sons they could come with me.

I set out with both boys jogging alongside me.

As we start to climb the trail, a day moon is rising in the late afternoon sky. The combination of the light and shadow are beautiful. I look back over my shoulder. Oliver has started to walk, but Julian is less than a quarter of a mile behind me and still running!

I'm looking back at my future.

We head up a trail between two sets of power lines. They offer a striking contrast to the tranquil scene unfolding beneath them. At this time of year it is warm and inviting, but in the winter it's an icy tundra accessible only by snowshoe, cross-country skis, or snowmobile. There are scores of animal footprints scurrying off in every direction, and beautiful red berries provide the only color for miles—"naught-naught berries" is what Julian and Oliver call them, because you're not allowed to eat them. But in the summer when the trees come back to life, frog ponds spawn tadpoles, bears cross the trail looking for berries and marking their territory, wildflowers bloom everywhere, and the rains leave giant mud puddles for the wildlife, our dogs, and sometimes our children to cool off in.

Last summer, while picking raspberries with his brother and me, Julian turned to me and asked, "I didn't ever meet Grand-pops, did I?"

"Sure you did. We have pictures of him holding you when you were a baby. And one time I took you into New York City to sur-prise him at Thanksgiving," I responded, trying to pump up their relationship.

"I know, but I wish I'd known him when I was this age because then I'd remember him," he replied.

"I know," I said.

"I never met him!" blurted Oliver, not wanting to be left out.

"No, you didn't, Ollie," I said. "He died before you were born."

"Are you sorry he died?" asked Julian.

"No, I'm not," I answered. "The dying wasn't so bad. I felt very close to him when he was dying. It's times like this that I miss him most."

Running now with both boys, surrounded by such beauty, it's hard not to think about Dad and how much he would have enjoyed this scene. He's missing out on so much. Climbing Cata-mount Mountain, picking berries, swimming in the river, running on trails through the woods, he would have loved doing these sort of things with us.

And then I see him . . .

He is so close, I feel I could reach out and touch him. A giant buck with a full rack, standing in the middle of the trail. He is beautiful, magisterial. His towering antlers seem as high as a church. I've never seen anything make the act of standing still seem like such a powerful motion. He is about thirty feet away from me. I start walking toward him. Because the woods are hunted so frequently, deer (especially the males) tend to disappear at the first sign of any human activity. This guy doesn't budge.

I close the distance between us by half and stop. Neither of us moves. We remain frozen like that, just staring into each other's eyes. Minutes pass like days. I start to feel my old friend eternity returning. Suddenly, he turns back in the direction from which he came and in two, maybe three leaps he is gone from sight. I have to resist the urge to chase after him.

I know the buck isn't my father, but a messenger—what Native Americans would call an emissary from the spirit world. Alone, standing in the deafening silence he left in his wake, I call out to him, not out of sorrow but in wonder, "Who are you, where are you going?"

When the boys catch up to me, it is on the tip of my tongue to tell them about the sighting. But I never do. That is the one thing I've kept completely to myself until now.

11

The Serenity Prayer

LESSONS ON FAITH AND GOD

IN HER *MORNINGS AND MOURNING*, E. M. Broner writes that her father, a well-known journalist, after reading the obituaries would say, "Look, somebody wonderful lived." He could have been talking about my father. I've never known a man more loved by so many than my father. So now I have two fears about finishing this book. The first one is simple: when I end the book, I worry my relationship with my father will end with it.

Broner wrote about another aspect of her experience that I resonated with. Broner's father asked for a daily Kaddish, the Jewish prayer for the dead. The problem is that only Orthodox synagogues offer a daily Kaddish, and Orthodox Jews don't allow women to say Kaddish.

Broner has called around looking for daily services and has met with the same resistance everywhere she calls. Desperate, she has tried every synagogue listed in the Manhattan phone book. One had a name that began with "Young":

> Young I think. That might be a youthful congregation and they're nearby. I phone.

"Do you have daily services?"

"For what purpose, may I ask?" The secretary doesn't sound very youthful.

"For me," I say, "to mourn my father."

"Oh no," says the secretary. "We do not allow our women to mourn." I picture their women with brimming eyes and fixed smiles.

"But what if they're in mourning?"

"There are professional mourners," she tells me, "for just such a purpose. You hire them."

"No, it's for me to do," I tell her.

"Not with us it isn't," she says. "Also a warning. You'll have a hard time getting an Amen." She pronounces it in Hebrew, "Ah-main."

The second mystery of the day in the lexicon of worship.

The secretary was right.

I would learn that, from certain quarters, when I rose to speak the Mourners Prayer, there would be a silence at each of the four or five places where the congregation was required to say Amen. The prayer was, therefore, regarded as null and void, my father dishonored.

Broner's experience raises the other fear I have about finishing this book. I worry that this book, my mourner's prayer, will disgrace my father rather than honor him; that there will be people who, when they read my mourning pages, will not say "Amen."

This chapter looks at how faith and prayer can help us face the unfamiliar. It takes courage to grieve and to face our feelings (and fears) openly and honestly. Sometimes prayer is simply a declaration of our willingness to take this journey into our pain and sorrow and to recover.

My father's favorite spiritual refrain was not "Amen." It was "I call." Dad was a student of many religions, but poker was unquestionably his favorite. He was part of a poker game that spanned forty years. They played every Sunday. Not unlike synagogue, players came and went but the core group stuck together. Old friends died. New ones joined. Dad's best friend Jack Blumenthal's death hit him hardest. Grief is simpler in poker. There it takes only five to make a minyan, instead of the ten men required at synagogue to say the most sacred prayers.

There is no Jesus hanging on a cross in my home, or mezuzah in the doorpost of my house to remind me of my faith. However, I do have a blown-up photograph of Dad's last big pot. When Dad was in the hospital in November before he died, his buddies moved the game there. They played it in the nurses' conference room across from my father's room. Fortunately, someone brought a camera.

In the photograph Dad is wearing his plaid wool bathrobe, the same blue and green one that my wife, Dana, now wears. His arms are extended so far out in front of him that he's almost prostrate as his hands, cupped around a pot of red, blue, and yellow chips—no whites, which means the bidding started high—pull his winnings to him. The expression on his face is one of pure joy and hunger, and there is wildness in his eyes. It is that crazed look of blind devotion worn by only the most fanatic believers when they are at worship. You see it on the faces of the men and women in the Bible scenes Michelangelo painted on the ceiling of the Sistine Chapel. Sometimes you see it at a rock concert.

Some might consider this passage blasphemous, but not Dad. For my father, poker wasn't about worshipping false gods, it was about tradition.

What If I Don't Know How to Pray?

The first time I said Kaddish for my father was during the High Holy Days after he died. I took his prayer book and my son Julian with me. Spanning centuries, the recitation of Kaddish is a sacred bond linking sons to their fathers and a younger generation to its people and its Torah. It lifts up both the soul of the deceased as well as the soul of the person who recites it.

Listening to the service with Julian on my lap, I was haunted by memories of sitting in temple with my own father. I dreaded going to synagogue with Dad. It always felt more about appearances than about God. During the service, Julian's reaction shocked me. He loved it, especially the singing. Initially, I was ambivalent about bringing him. I was afraid he would become too bored or fidgety and disrupt the services. Instead, I was reminded of my father's earliest memory of attending prayer services with his father. He wrote about it in a passage of a manuscript he intended to publish before he died.

> As a five year old, I didn't know who the Jews were or why we were there. Nevertheless, the special robes worn by the cantor and the rabbi and, above all, the special melodies of the High Holy Days—more solemn than those of the Sabbath, and daily liturgies—stirred me deeply. They still do, especially the pivotal prayer that expresses their central theme—our mortality.

An odd feeling came over me. As if I was interrupting a conversation between my son and his grandfather.

Many men express extreme discomfort with the spiritual aspects of death and dying. What's more, even if they're able to overcome these feelings and embrace their faith or the idea of spirituality, the whole concept of prayer often raises people's insecurities. These concerns used to bring up my own feelings of inadequacy until a colleague told me about one of his clients, a recovering alcoholic, who came to see him explicitly because of the trouble he was having with the spiritual part of his recovery, what AA calls the "God stuff." He was especially unnerved at the thought of using prayer and meditation to help him stay sober. He said he didn't know how to pray, that he'd never done it.

Then one time he came late for an appointment very upset with himself. He said he was ashamed of his behavior. He'd really hit bottom with his addiction—all his problems seemed to be crashing in on him. He was desperate to see his counselor and got stuck in traffic. Instead of using what he'd learned in AA about taking things "one day at a time" and "easy does it," he became furious. He was hammering his steering wheel with his fist, cursing God, and shouting at the car in front of him "Jesus Christ almighty" and a litany of other epithets. My colleague interrupted him. "I thought you said you didn't know how to pray?" he asked.

The point is that our prayers don't need to read like scripture or sound like poetry in order to reach a compassionate or understanding "other," including the being or presence we call God. It's okay to cry out in protest.

Each activity of daily life in which we stretch ourselves on behalf of others (or express regret about not having done so) is what writer Richard Foster refers to as a "prayer of action"—the times when we scrimp and save in order to get the children something special; the times when we share our car with others on rainy mornings, leaving early to get them to work on time; the times when we keep up a correspondence with a friend or answer one last telephone call when we're dead tired at night. Those actions and many more like them are what Foster calls "lived prayers."

This is what we humans are trying to capture with our prayers and religious symbols, the human spirit prevailing in a world of pain. For some, only the concept of a being or presence as omnipotent as God is large enough to heal the scars of violence and abuse or the shame that stems from an undying need for a parent or unconditional love.

Even if we do not consider ourselves religious, we all must rely upon something to carry us through our grief and despair. Life is full of sorrow, but it is also full of joy. As the writer Julia Cameron explains, for many of us "it is hard to be both large enough and small enough to hold the range of life. Without a spiritual connection to something larger than ourselves, we lose our bearings, our beings, our sense of scale." For these reasons, I always encourage clients to explore sources of spiritual support for their recovery, which could range from God to Buddha to a less traditional higher power to a felt connection to nature.

God's Country

"Daddy, are you missing Grandpops?" The first time Julian asked me that, I did a double take, as he wasn't even quite three. "Yes I am, very much," I answered. "Well, you don't have to worry," he said, "because I've seen him." When I asked him where he'd seen his grandfather, he said, "In my room at night." Now, there are pictures of my father up all over our house—including one of him as a child that hangs in our children's room—so of course Julian sees him all the time. But I don't think that's what he meant. And although I didn't give it much thought at the time, I never forgot the way he said it. I asked him if Grandpops had said anything to him. "Yes, he said to give you this hug," he answered, and threw his tiny arms around me. I squeezed him tightly and said, "You give this hug to Grandpops next time you see him."

"Much of life can never be explained, only witnessed," wrote Naomi Rachel Remen. Dad was never interested in looking for proof of an afterlife or the existence of a spirit world. He didn't need to; he got such a high from living in this one. And I don't need to look for any further signs of one either to affirm my connection to him, because, in one of the oddest twists of fate, I've found myself surrounded by him in the small New England village that my wife and I have settled in.

Heath is an amazingly beautiful place. When I told an old neighbor of mine in a nearby town—a farmer who lives on a swatch of land that looks like something the Israelites saw on the other side of the river Jordan after forty years of wandering in the desert—that we were moving there he said: "Heath, that's God's country!"

At 2,300 feet above sea level, Heath enjoys the highest elevation of any town in Massachusetts. However, in addition to boasting the most burned clutches per hundred people in the state, Heath has one other claim to fame: it is where my father's mentor theologian Reinhold Niebuhr wrote and first delivered his best known words, the serenity prayer. Niebuhr and his family spent their summers here (the cottage he lived in has an historic marker in front of it). At least once during each stay, Niebuhr would be invited to give a sermon at the Heath Union Church.

In the summer of 1943 he wrote a prayer for the occasion. Moved by its words, a colleague in attendance asked him if he might have a copy of it. Niebuhr obliged by handing him his notes with the prayer written on them. Eventually it made its way to the (then) fledgling Alcoholics Anonymous, and the group asked Niebuhr's permission to use it as a staple of their spiritual "fellowship." Now there are T-shirts with the prayer printed on it for sale at Peter's General Store in North Heath.

Growing up, Niebuhr's was a name I was taught to revere. Dad studied with Niebuhr's brother Richard for two years at Yale's divinity school and used to sit in on his lectures when Niebuhr was teaching at Union Theological Seminary in New York City and Dad was finishing up his Ph.D. at Columbia. Later he had the thrill of teaching on the same faculty with him when Niebuhr came to Princeton as a visiting professor.

So when one January my neighbors, Cal and Jan, discovered that Niebuhr's daughter, Elisabeth Sifton, was going to be the guest of honor at the Heath Historical Society's annual dinner meeting at the elementary school, they called me on the phone and said, "Find a baby-sitter, we're going and you're coming with us!"

Apparently, it was a milestone anniversary of the serenity prayer, and one of the historical society members decided that it would be a good opportunity to invite her to speak. Elisabeth graciously accepted. I had never been to one of these gatherings in our town before. So not only was it an opportunity to learn more about the man whose thoughts and writing had such a profound influence on my father, it was a chance to become more acclimated to the local culture in Heath.

Dinner was followed by the customary giant vanilla sheet cake with chocolate frosting, although surely none that had ever been prepared with a copy of the serenity prayer written in blue and green icing across the top. The speaker even commented that she'd had just about every kind of encounter with the serenity prayer one could imagine—coffee mugs, T-shirts, plaques, quilts, posters, and so on—but that she'd never eaten it before. Personally, I was hoping to get a piece of acceptance, serenity, or wisdom. But unfortunately, by the time the line got around to me, I had to settle for a slice with her dad's name on it. I suppose, in a manner of speaking, you could say I got to taste all three, as I got to take a bite of Niebuhr himself!

I've spent nineteen years reciting the serenity prayer at the beginning of Al-Anon meetings. My mother continues to suffer from alcoholism, as she has throughout most of my life. When I decided to marry my partner, Dana, I became very anxious about my mother's drinking. Unsure of how to handle the presence of alcohol at our wedding and apprehensive about how she might behave, I sought advice from my beloved friend and colleague, Roget Lockard, who is an expert on addictions. After listening patiently to my dilemma, Roget asked me to entertain the following scenario: "Imagine, Jon, if tomorrow morning you went out to your mailbox and discovered a telegram. You opened it and read: 'Dear Jonathan, I am sorry; it is not in the stars for your mother to get better. Love, God.'"

As he spoke those words, I fought back tears. As never before, I understood the well-worn words of Niebuhr's prayer (as adapted by AA): "God, grant me the serenity to accept the things I can not change, the courage to change the things I can, and the wisdom to know the difference." I got, in that moment, that my mother and I were equally powerless over her drinking, and that I could not, and never would be able to, "fix" her. I often recall this moment as I work with addicted clients who struggle with letting go of their substance—it both keeps me connected to my client and restrains me from engaging in futile rescue missions.

AA's rendition of Niebuhr's prayer was also a mantra of my father's. He heard it repeated many times at AA meetings he attended. Dad began going to AA to research a paper he was writing on morality and religion. However, what started out as an academic endeavor was quickly transformed into a personal sojourn. Dad discovered in AA a peace and tranquillity that had always eluded him. Of all the talking and drug therapy he tried over the years, this was the first intervention that seemed to genuinely help him manage his explosive temper. During the period of his life he attended most consistently, he began referring to himself as a "rageaholic." The effects were dramatic. He was more present, patient, and lighthearted. In a word, it made him more *human*. And for that reason I'm extremely grateful for AA's version of Niebuhr's prayer (and protective of it).

Elisabeth bridles that her father didn't fuss when AA altered the prayer's wording in the second clause, which originally read "courage to change what should be changed" to, in AA's rendering, "courage to change the things I can." She rightly argues that "there are circumstances that should be changed yet may seem beyond our powers to alter, and these are the circumstances under which the prayer is most needed." She refers to Nelson

Mandela and the twenty-five years he spent in prison during the struggle to end apartheid in South Africa. This, she says, is an example of the kind of strength and courage her father had in mind when he wrote the prayer.

The word "should" is not found anywhere in AA or Al-Anon's spiritual lexicon. But I don't think the move away from that word was to make the job of prayer easier, as Elisabeth fears, but was to avoid taking a stand that assumes any of us has a corner on the truth or that our own perspective and interpretation of events is the only one we can trust. This was something Elisabeth's father was constantly cautioning against.

In a lecture my father gave on the eve of his retirement, his last delivered on Princeton's campus after forty years of teaching, Dad shared the following memory of Niebuhr:

> On a Sunday morning Niebuhr was preaching in James Chapel at Union Theological Seminary. It was, as usual when he preached, standing room only. In the course of the sermon he told us that he attended John Dewey's ninetieth birthday celebration that week and, of course, Dewey spoke. Among the things he said was "The greatest sin we can commit is not to trust our fellow man." Niebuhr spread his arms so that the sleeves of his robes dangling from them looked like eagles wings. The effect was heightened by his bald head, aquiline nose, and piercing eyes. "That's good, but not good enough," he growled. Then he pointed a finger at us and said: "The greatest sin we can commit is not to trust our fellow man, when we trust ourselves!"

Niebuhr's message seems especially poignant given events taking place in the world today. However, this sort of struggle is not only a political battle; it is, as Niebuhr understood, a deeply personal and spiritual one.

When my father first encountered Niebuhr's work, he was having what he referred to as a "breakdown," but what I prefer to think of as a crisis of self-comprehension. He was lost and drifting, questioning his faith and struggling with a lot of painful family experience. The influence that Niebuhr's thinking had on my father was so profound that he thought of converting to Christianity.

Ultimately, what my father did was return to his own faith, where he tried to find in Judaism what it was that had drawn him to Niebuhr in the first place. He found it in the thinking of the Jewish theologian Martin Buber.

Buber's beliefs can be summed up in a phrase from his *Tales of the Hassidim* (a kind of *1001 Arabian Nights* for the kosher set): "A man stands alone and cannot sing. Another man stands with him and the first man can also sing." Buber's concept of I-Thou incorporates many of the principles that are bedrock to Niebuhr's Christianity; for example, embracing the "Otherness" of other human beings as our own and placing more importance on what we do and experience here on Earth than on what reward we might experience in heaven or the next life.

In Mitch Albom's *The Five People You Meet in Heaven*, one of the characters tells Eddie, the story's protagonist, "Each of us was in your life for a reason. You may not have known the reason at the time, and that is what heaven is for. For understanding your life on earth." The wonderful thing about the angels Eddie encounters in heaven is that they're *human*. They lose their tempers, get hungry, scold God; they are egotistical, testy, or impatient in turn, make mistakes and regret them. Still they go on doggedly blundering toward heaven, trying to leave the world a better place than they found it.

Albom's is a good story because it's about the beauty of humanity. How we relate to one another and how we struggle with one another. All from a place of love. It's good to tell stories like that. It's good to hear stories like that. These kinds of stories are good for the soul.

.   .   .

The year my father was hired to teach as an instructor, Princeton had just begun to open its doors to Jews. During his interview, the head of the department said, "I hope you understand, Mr. Diamond, that this is a white, Protestant, Republican institution." My father replied, "I can forgive it the first two, but not the latter."

Like my father, I'm very much the *tikkun* Jew. A "make the world better" Jew. Not a religious one. Nonetheless, there I was five years after my father's death, writing a book about fathers and sons, listening to the daughter of one of my father's intellectual heroes—a man who was arguably the greatest theologian of his generation—speaking in my son's elementary school in the heart of Yankee New England about a beloved prayer, Christianity, and her meditations on religious commitment and political engagement.

At the end of her talk, as Elisabeth wiped a sentimental tear from her eye, I felt closer to my own father than I could have if I had been sitting in his yeshiva in the Flatbush section of Brooklyn listening to the liturgy and singing of the Orthodox cantors he grew up with.

Elisabeth concluded the evening with a different set of words from her father—a short riff on the central Christian text from the Second Corinthians about faith and hope. I was so inspired by them, I want to pass them on here:

Nothing worth doing can be achieved in a lifetime; therefore we must be saved by hope. Nothing that is true or beautiful or good makes complete sense in any immediate context of history; therefore we must be saved by faith. Nothing that we do, however virtuous, can be accomplished alone; therefore we are saved by love.

The Pilgrimage

In November 1992, my father traveled to the Middle East on a retirement trip he had long planned. As the time drew near, his red blood cell count declined, and his fatigue got worse. It took a transfusion to get the blood cells back to the point where he could make the strenuous journey. Every day he explored another temple, one marvel after another. For him the climax came early one morning, when he climbed five thousand feet to the top of Mount Sinai. He sang a prayer celebrating Moses receiving the Torah there. It was a melody his father had taught him. As the sun rose, the barren rocks changed from one startling color to another.

Gazing at the Promised Land stretched out before him, he thought of the dazzling combination of technological genius and aesthetic creativity of the Jewish people and culture that occupied it. Unified by a religious vision. The culture presenting an endless parade of natural objects that symbolize the ultimate mystery: a sacred universe.

He grieved over the history of his people, with its massacres and exiles. But standing on this holiest of grounds, he couldn't help wondering how, two thousand years after Moses received the tablets from God, this chosen people could still find themselves at war. In 1932, when my father was eight years old, Hitler was gaining power in Europe. He taught the doctrine of the master race, which thought Jews inferior. This notion repulsed my father. He devoted his career to standing up for the rights of the innocent and the voice of the oppressed.

After years of fighting the good fight, he arrived at the conclusion that none of us is immune to the basic type of what he called egocentricity that leads to acts of guilt and to violence. A fact that the history of the Jewish state has actualized. We all can become, in Albert Camus' terms, both victim and executioner. The pain of each is real and requires acknowledgment; the failure of each is real and requires accountability.

Like Moses standing on the threshold of the Promised Land but not allowed to enter it, my father was never able to shed this cycle of abuse. Hard as he tried to change when it came to finding a home without violence and fear, he would forever be a wanderer in the desert.

12

Parting Words

I always thought that cemeteries were a waste of space,
until we buried my father in one.

—Nick Connolly

ALL OF US HAVE HAD the experience of shifting uncomfortably in
our seats as the rabbi, priest, or minister makes the dearly
departed out to be a saint or at least a much better person than
he or she was. But we all do this in ways large and small. And we
need to. It's important to have alternative stories of people and
events, because you have to imagine something before you can
do it. Just as the novelist writes about something that's better or
more interesting than circumstances as they now are, in grief we
don't just try to imagine the dead going to a better world, we
imagine our being in a better world with them. We write this
alternative story in the hope of taking a step toward it and casting our experience in a better or at least a different light.

Like a good story, the words we share at a funeral are meant
to help people construct narratives that give new meaning to
their experience and their lives. Even the gravestones and other

markers we plant do not endure as objects but as presences. They make our stories come alive and seem more real. And as we learned from *The Velveteen Rabbit*, once we are real, our lives and the stories we tell about them never seem broken or ugly except to those who don't understand.

"Just Remember I Loved You All"

Nick talked about the ways his father's service helped him re-story their relationship and the forgiveness he felt afterward:

> My father was really into musicals, so at his funeral we sang a lot of songs that he liked. Including his favorite, "Sunrise, Sunset" from *Fiddler on the Roof*. He loved that song. I know it's sappy, but it's such a great song for a funeral.
>
> I got in touch with more forgiveness during those days than I thought possible. I have a difficult time with the Catholic Church and so much of what it stands for. But sitting in that church, I was able to forgive them too. Because at least they provided a container for our grief— the sureness of that place and their rituals and cere- monies just made it easier. I actually found it reassuring, which surprised me.
>
> Even the ugly cemetery, which I absolutely hated— the one that wouldn't allow us to plant trees because it got in the way of mowing their lawns—I was even grateful to have that because it was a place I could go and see my father. Which, until he died, was something I never imag- ined myself doing.

A year after Crash died, Nick and his siblings borrowed another tradition from their Jewish friends; they had a grave unveiling. Nick said he didn't think there were many Jews buried in Saint Patrick's cemetery (which I thought was a pretty safe hypothesis), but they decided to perform this ceremony anyway. Together, the children had a black granite bench made for their father inscribed with the last words Crash spoke to them as they were assembled around his deathbed: "Just remember I loved you all."

Nowadays, Nick talks to Crash all the time. Nick described his last visit to the cemetery: "I asked him for his sense of humor, his intelligence, and his ability to engage with people who didn't like him. Sometimes I'm just so totally full of my father, it's as if he's right here with me—literally, right here with me—and then we get to laugh and sing songs together. It's great."

The conversations aren't always this pleasant or easy. There are times when he argues with his father for not taking better care of his health or when he recalls the drunken phone calls in the middle of the night. "But," said Nick, "whenever I get up from that bench, no matter how angry or upset I am with him, my father always has the last word."

Amazing Grace

My client Ervin went with his Aunt Celina to get a headstone for his father's grave. As his father had requested, they had the first verse of "Amazing Grace" inscribed on it and mourners sang it at his service:

> Amazing grace! How sweet the sound
> That saved a wretch like me.
> I once was lost, but now am found,
> Was blind, but now I see.

You can't sing hymns without being moved. Grown men, books and mouths open wide, often bawl like babies. Written by the hand of God, hymns are passwords to the soul. "Balm in

Gilead," "Sojourner's Battle Hymn," "Rivers of Babylon," "Precious Lord, Take My Hand"—these are the anthems of angels. The words speak of the power of love and faith. For those of us in mourning or who carry the burden of another type of soul wound, the music helps us to inhabit the parts of ourselves we have long since abandoned or given up on.

For therapists, suffering is no abstraction. Because of the work we do, we often see people at their most grievous and formidable moments. People, at these times, are severely wounded. They feel fragmented, like they are missing parts of themselves. Their situations seem hopeless and their lives beyond mending. If one sees, to paraphrase Bernie Siegel, one can witness how noble and beautiful people are when they're going through these painful experiences. One sees their strength and wholeness.

Prior to the funeral, Ervin's relatives kept commenting how much his voice sounded like his father's. Ervin could hear it, too. Singing at his father's graveside, Ervin experienced grace. He was delirious with it. Suddenly, his father's voice just started pouring out of him. And as he stood in the circle, while his father's coffin was lowered into the grave, an odd feeling came over him. It was one he'd never felt before. But he recognized it right away. For the first time in his life, Ervin felt whole.

Playing Catch

Stan's cemetery is a beautiful place; it's out in the country surrounded by farmland. It's a mix of old and new. There are gravestones from the mid-nineteenth century. His brother who helped Stan die plans to be buried there in plots they bought ahead of time. Every time Lenny returns to Rochester, he visits his father's grave. One summer when he and his wife, Sarah, were going, he asked his oldest son if he would like to join them. And to his surprise, Charlie, just ten years old at the time, said yes. On his way out the door, Lenny called to him, "Charlie, let's bring our mitts."

When they arrived at the cemetery, father and son started playing catch over Stan's gravestone. Lenny was catching the ball and throwing it back to his son as he was talking to Sarah about the week's activities. When he looked over, however, he saw his son's lips moving. "Charlie, what are you saying?" asked Lenny. But Charlie just brushed his father off as if to say, "Leave me alone, I'm talking to Grandpa." Lenny realized his son was having a conversation with his grandfather.

"Everything good we've ever been given is ours forever," writes Naomi Rachel Remen. The memory of standing on his father's grave, playing catch with his son Charlie, will remain with Lenny for a long time. What the heart can hold is never lost.

Many poets and writers describe the moment of death as a return to wholeness. For Nick and Lenny this meant being able to reclaim their fathers' spirits to watch over and guide them; for Ervin it was being able to reclaim himself; for Sam, my client who brought the copy of Simon Wiesenthal's *The Sunflower* to his first session, it was rediscovering his relationship with his mother; for Jesse, the boy whose father, Gere, threw him across the room in a fit of rage, it was having a whole father again; for Gere, it was becoming one. The less broken have to take care of the more broken. I learned that from my clients.

The Batterers' Group

My father's parting message to me wasn't a word, it was a gesture.

During one of Dad's last hospitalizations, he was desperately trying to get through on the phone to a batterers' program to set up an intake for himself. Two weeks prior he had been at my doctoral defense. The trip had taken a lot out of him. He had decided to risk it because he wasn't sure he would be able to make it to my graduation in August. He wasn't sure he would be strong enough or if he would be alive. At that particular moment, Dad wasn't concerned about dying; he was on the phone.

Just before my defense, I had gotten a call from Denise, Dad's wife. She told me Dad had hit her. He hadn't struck her in fifteen years, but it had happened again. Dad blamed it on the steroids. That same week in the middle of the night, he had taken apart his study in what his doctor described as a "'roid rage"—the side effects of the medication he used to keep up his strength and energy. And in fact, the medication he was taking, if taken in large enough doses, can make people do crazy things.

But as Denise explained, even though it had been years since Dad had struck her, he had never stopped breaking and slamming things in the house when angry. Once she had to call the police, which my brother and I knew nothing about.

It didn't matter to me if the meds did play a role. His doctor's solution was to prescribe Ativan, a sedative known for combatting anxiety. Its addictive traits made it not the best choice for Dad, but I suppose his doctor assumed that at this stage of the game, drug dependency was the least of my father's problems. Regardless, those of us who knew my father best understood that the medication wasn't responsible for his violence.

Denise wasn't sure what she was going to do. Leave or stay. But she wanted me to know. I told her I thought she should press charges this time, but I would support any decision she made. Denise's call didn't surprise me, but that didn't lessen the shock it caused. After I hung up the phone, I felt sick to my stomach. I'd like to say that after all the therapy he and I did together, all the therapy that Dad did on his own, and all those twelve-step meetings, my father never lashed out at anyone in that way again. But that's not how the story ended. Real events don't have endings, only the stories we tell about them do.

Dad called me later. "Do you still want me to come up?" he asked. I answered yes, but I was ambivalent. I felt as if I was rewarding him. However, the fact remained that I desperately wanted him to be there. I understood it might be our last opportunity to spend this kind of time together. While I meant what I said to my stepmother about pressing charges, I was also feeling resentful because, once again, the fallout from my father's marriage was interfering with another important event in my life. I rationalized my decision by telling myself that Denise could use the time alone and would be relieved to be rid of Dad for a few days, which I know was true.

My father was on his best behavior that weekend. Part of it was the occasion. Part of it was that he was always at his best, as well as his most contrite and accommodating, after one of his violent episodes. Sometime during our visit he thanked me for being so supportive of Denise. "I didn't do it for her, I did it for myself," I replied. I surprised myself with the force I spoke the words with.

The next morning at breakfast, Dad was manic. The night before, he'd watched a program on TV about battering. It was on *20/20* or some other news program like it. Dad had called the 800 number flashed on the screen at the end of the segment to find out where men could get help. It turned out to be the number of an agency that ran a batterers' group in Trenton, New Jersey. "What are the odds of that!" he said excitedly. I tried not to state the obvious, which is that a therapist in private practice should have the names and numbers of these programs in his Rolodex. As far as I was concerned, he'd been in need of this type of group his entire life.

Dad was in a panic. He'd been trying to get through to the batterers' program all morning. He'd left several messages, but no one had called him back. I know he was driven by fear. Fear of dying alone. Fear of Denise leaving him. Fear of his sons abandoning him in shame. He was human. But he was also genuinely remorseful. All my life, Dad never stopped trying to get it right. The results weren't always what either of us wanted, but he tried to do the right thing. And maybe this time his terror wasn't just of dying, or even of death, but, as the poet Sharon Olds wrote about her father, of some cry kept hidden deep inside him all of his life and there were only months left.

I had always identified with the victims of my father's violence, especially my mother. And despite my often strained relationship with my stepmother, whenever Dad became violent or abusive, I always sided with her. However, sitting in his hospital room watching him try to get hold of the group leader, for the first time in my life I found myself pulling for him. And it felt good. "You can do this, I know you can," I thought to myself, cheering him on. He finally did get through to a staff person in the program and, much to his relief, was able to set up an initial appointment. After he was cleared to leave the hospital, he went dutifully to his weekly sessions.

Whenever my father's impressive list of affiliations and groups he belonged to are mentioned, this one—the last one he joined—is never included. However, it was, in my opinion, the most important of all, and it is the one I'm most proud of.

I'm also very clear that my father's participation in a ten-week group did not make up for his past behavior toward my mother or my stepmother. Within Judaism, the person who confesses and repents atones only for transgressions between human beings and God. God cannot forgive you or hand you a clean slate for other good deeds you do, even important ones. For transgressions between one individual and another, atonement is achieved only by reconciling with the person who has been offended. For Dad, that would have required a much greater commitment of time, and time was the one thing my father had run out of.

My father didn't like speaking about his experience at the group. Shortly before he died, I tried to get him to talk about it.

"I don't know why you keep bringing that up, Jon!" Dad shouted, sounding very beleaguered and upset. "It's the part of my life I hate most, and I carry a tremendous amount of shame and remorse because of it."

"I know, Dad," I said, mustering all the compassion I could. "Because now that you do, I no longer have to."

My father's parting act was what my son's kindergarten teacher calls an "apology of action." This time, Dad wasn't just apologizing for his violent and abusive behavior, he was actually making an effort to do something about it.

Instead of threatening to destroy me, for the first time in my life, the winds of my father's anger were trying to protect and shelter me.

REFLECTION

———

"Do-Over!!!"

One of the hardest things for me to accept is that I don't just channel my father's love for me when I'm missing him. His presence is felt each time I tear into Dana, Julian, or Oliver with a flash of sarcasm in a way that . . . well . . . in a way that does just what the word "sarcasm" means—the tearing of flesh.

I felt his presence when I lost my temper at Oliver for emptying an entire tube of toothpaste on the cherrywood floor in the dining room, the bathroom walls, his hair, and his shirt and pants two minutes before we were supposed to leave for Julian's swimming class (which we were already running late for). My response was to throw him in the bathtub, clothes and all, and wash off the toothpaste with shampoo while he cried hysterically, oblivious to whether the burning minty gel was getting in his eyes or on his outstretched tongue; ranting and raving the whole time about how fed up I am with this kind of behavior. Until finally Julian, just five years old, restored the situation (and me) to sanity by saying, "Mommy never acts like that when she's angry."

When my father shows up in our lives (and me) at these moments, it reminds me of playing four square on the playground at recess when I was in the third and fourth grades. When the ball landed on the line, all the children would fight over whether it was "in play" or "out of bounds." Things got ugly fast. There was pushing and shoving. The arguing would

210

reach a fever pitch and then out of the blue some kid would yell *"Do-over!!!"*—said like one word, causing the whole landscape and everyone in it to freeze. Time stopped, like deer and other wildlife in the forest when a gunshot rings. But when it was over, instead of pandemonium and chaos, the game resumed as if nothing had happened.

I want the anger that surfaces in my interactions with Julian and Oliver to be an opportunity for a "do-over," not a reenactment. There is nothing more awful than attacking your own kids. It's the worst feeling I know, shouting at these forty-pound little beings with their huge, trusting brown eyes. It is, as Anne Lamott so colorfully puts it, "like bitch-slapping E.T." There are other ways I prefer to be remembered as a father.

13

Fathering without Fathers

Out beyond ideas of right doing and wrongdoing, there
is a field. I'll meet you there.

—RUMI

THE PRESSURES OF BEING A PARENT are equal to any pressure on
Earth. To be a conscious parent and really look to another
being's mental and physical health is a responsibility that most of
us find difficult to bear. Throughout the writing of this book, I've
kept in mind three groups of male readers: those who already
have lost a father; those whose fathers are alive, but aged and
dying; and those who are fathers themselves. This chapter speaks
directly to the men who are trying to raise sons themselves.

It requires a lot of nurturing to parent others. It is hard for a
woman to provide mothering to her children in the absence of a
strong maternal presence in her life, or for a man to provide
fathering without the protective presence of his father's love to
guide him. But we are fooling ourselves if we think our fathers
exist now only in the photographs on our desks or in the armful
of memories we still hold tight.

Reflecting upon his dad's death, one of the things Nick Connolly said he would miss most was his father's special way of phrasing things and how his daughter wouldn't get to experience his influence directly in her life:

> I don't know what the right word is, but he had these incantations, like the "do you know why you're wonderful" thing. He had hundreds of these kinds of little daily sayings. One he said to us all the time I actually caught my daughter saying to me. I can't remember what we were talking about, but I was putting her to bed and she looked at me and said, "Okay, Dad, you're on your own." It totally startled me. After I got over my surprise I said, "Wait, you're not my father—that's what he used to say!" And then I realized, I must say that all the time. How else would a six-year-old kid say something so weird as "you're on your own"? And, of course, I *do* say it all the time. And now Livia says it, too. So there he is. It's like he lives on inside everything I do. His presence influenced who I was and his absence still influences who I am.

"Our lives are shaped as much by those who leave us as they are by those who stay," wrote the author Hope Edelman. Nick's exchange with his daughter brought him face-to-face with this wonderful and often painful truth. However, even sons who have been estranged or cut off from their fathers cannot escape the power of these paternal relationships, as demonstrated in the following story about fatherhood and living blues legend Buddy Guy.

In a radio interview, Buddy Guy told a story about the son he sired but didn't raise. As the boy grew into young manhood, Buddy sought him out, hoping they could become closer. His son had also become a guitarist, but he wanted nothing to do with Buddy or his brand of music. He had his own rock star idol:

Prince. When the young man anonymously sought a teacher who could help him to emulate his idol, he was told that if he wanted to sound like Prince, he needed to understand how to play guitar like Jimi Hendrix; and in order to understand Jimi Hendrix, the teacher said, he needed to learn about Hendrix's biggest musical influence: the guitarist Buddy Guy.

The message this story holds is that a man cannot show up for his role as a father without coming face-to-face with the fathering he received. Try as we might, we cannot hide from our past, especially one that is wrapped in anger, loss, and sorrow. We need to have faith that the present is big enough to hold the past. And while we cannot choose much of what happens to us in our lives, we can choose how we respond to what happens.

Breaking the Chain

There was only one time I was grateful for the parts of my father's temper I inherited. When my son Julian was around four months old, we tried an encore of the wonderful visit to Princeton that we had enjoyed shortly after he was born. My father was not in good shape. Perhaps the joy of seeing his only grandson was, at this point, overshadowed by the knowledge that he was not going to watch him grow up. I'm not sure. What I do know is that while trying to cajole my father out of one of his angry moods, I asked him to be mindful of how loud he was getting as Julian was sleeping in my arms. My father, his voice dripping with sarcasm, said, "Knock it off, Jon, he's just a baby. Stop acting like he's so fucking precious!"

My wife, Dana, and I looked at each other in disbelief, and then I turned on my father like a lioness protecting her cub. "You will never ever talk that way around our son or you will never lay eyes on him again, do you understand?!" I said through gritted teeth, barely able to contain my rage. My father tried to backpedal, but I was too angry and upset to care. I retreated to the bedroom.

"We're leaving now," I said to Dana. Dad followed me downstairs. He said he didn't think what he'd said was so awful, but he was sorry if it upset me. "You're going to have to do a whole lot better than that, Dad!" I shot back. He begged us to stay. I was still fuming. And then he gave me a hug. Julian was still sleeping in my arms, so he had to wrap his arms around us both. I started crying, but managed to get one more "God damn it, Dad!" out between sobs. "I'm sorry. I'm truly sorry," he said while gently caressing the back of my head.

When I was growing up, my father was very demonstrative. He was always hugging and kissing me whenever he saw me. Some men have no memory of their dads hugging them, even as small children. As a teenager, I was shocked to learn that not every kid's father was a candidate for drug trials involving experimental medications with names like Preventafit or Stop-a-Rage. However, I was just as amazed to learn that dad's and my public displays of affection were not normal father-son behavior. Many adult sons, I've discovered, waited until they were twenty-five or thirty before hugging their fathers for the first time. Others have had to wait until their dads were on their deathbeds before introducing words like "hug," "kiss," and "touch" into their father-son lexicons.

Hugging is one of the best ways I can think of for a man to introduce hope into a strained or broken relationship with his father or to comfort him when he's dying. If it's something you're not accustomed to doing, it may feel awkward at first. But while it may not be easy, it is simple, and best of all, it's powerful.

If you are a young father, do not wait until you're on your deathbed to initiate this practice with your own son. Research shows that male toddlers are less than half as likely to be touched as their female counterparts. By the time boys turn seven or eight, they receive ten times less hugging, holding, caressing, and other forms of intimate contact than girls do, by both parents. By the time a boy is in his teens, virtually all expression of physical affection and intimacy ceases to exist.

Contrary to popular myth, men are relational creatures. We function at our best within the context of connected, supportive communities. If writing this book has taught me anything, it is that sons and their fathers both feel immense natural empathy for one another and yearn to develop closer, more loving relationships. This is especially true for young children and their fathers.

William Pollack concluded the same after years of researching men's relationships, which he later published in his best-seller *Real Boys*. A boy whose father stays close to him during infancy and early childhood benefits from this fundamental father-son connection for a lifetime. And this is as true for boys who were raised by stepfathers and other male parenting figures as it was for biological fathers and sons. Longitudinal studies show that fathers who remain close to their children in childhood rear sons who are better able to weather the turbulence of adolescence. Men whose fathers took a more active parenting role are also better able to compromise and to resolve conflicts, and they demonstrate a greater capacity for empathy.

As the poet and author Grace Paley writes, "Fathers are doing more fathering these days; and they've accomplished this by being more mothering." An exchange a friend of mine had with his father one week after his son was born drives this point home. Holding his newborn son lovingly in his arms, my friend asked his father if he would like a turn. His father's response was enthusiastic but his actions were more tentative. "I don't think I've ever held a baby this tiny before," his father said awkwardly, clutching his grandson. My friend was stunned by his father's remark. He found it both tender and chilling.

Honoring Your Father's Memory

There are other ways a son can honor his father's memory or re-story difficult ones through his own parenting style. First and foremost: *protect time with your son*. An earlier chapter discussed the importance of work to men's sense of identity and mourning and acknowledged how trendy it has become to throw around terms like "workaholism." However, this is a very real problem that affects many men and drastically interferes with their parenting.

Studies documenting the disappearance of our leisure time and the declining productivity of the American worker, despite the increased time we spend on the job, are missing the point. These studies are part of the problem. They are trying to demonstrate that less is more and that rest results in a physically healthier and more emotionally stable and productive workforce. However, it shouldn't matter what the impact is on the marketplace, because what is at stake is no less than the overall well-being of our sons and daughters and the future of our families and communities.

In order to have healthy, loving families, men need to be emotionally available to their spouses and children. Raising a family and caring for the needs of small children—or older ones, for that matter—takes a huge investment of time. Oftentimes, those needs are going to be in conflict with society's emphasis on work and career. While women are not supported any better than men in this endeavor, it is nevertheless expected and more socially acceptable for a woman, if she has the luxury, to opt out of the workforce or to cut back in order to stay at home with her children. A man who does so remains the exception, not the norm. Most men still feel that the best way to parent is to be a competent breadwinner rather than to spend time with their kids.

In addition to time constraints and succumbing to the increasing demands of work, William Pollack observes that some fathers resist getting closely involved in nurturing their sons because of the myths about these children becoming "momma's boys."

Many fathers fear that if they don't follow what Pollack calls the "Old Boy Code" by acting "tough" around their sons—and by pushing their boys to act strong and independent—their sons will become outcast sissies rather than real boys destined for success in the mainstream. This was an obstacle Lenny encountered during his childhood, despite the unusually close and tender relationship he enjoyed with his father:

> Growing up, both my parents wanted more for me than what they had for themselves and they saw a college education being the means to that end. However, they were a bit frustrated with my choices. I was a theater major. And I actually had some problems with my father when I was going down that path. I think there was first and foremost a fear of homosexuality—homophobia about my being involved with theater, because isn't everyone involved in theater gay, a lesbian, or a drug addict? I remember my last summer before I was going to go off to college being at the dinner table and my dad sort of losing it—rarely did he do so. But he made it very clear that he didn't want me to go "pussyfooting around with all those drama faggots." I think that's a quote. He had a hard time with it at first; it was just, I think, too much. Too different.

Lenny talked about this exchange with his dad with an unusual amount of compassion and understanding for his father's feelings, wrong as he believed them to be. This is a good example of how I counsel approaching father-son relations at the end of life. Don't ignore problems, but don't catastrophize either. Fix what is fixable, accept what isn't, and move on.

Therapy is a meaning-building activity. My own bias is that when done properly, it takes time and patience. However, while therapy is not a quick fix or solution for our problems, neither is it necessary to spend five years on the couch in order to bring healing to a difficult situation or relationship. I'm thinking of my work with Jesse and with Gere. The two of them were able to make remarkable inroads in a relatively brief period of time. Sometimes, even one or two sessions can help a family mend and move forward.

Long Day's Journey into Day

My father's last night at home before he and my mother separated for good was an awful memory that haunted me for years. My brother and I were playing a board game with our father. Mom, slurring her way through a speech she'd been waiting to deliver for the better part of twenty years, demanded that Dad leave. Dad protested at first but finally relented. Mom kept taunting him. She followed him into every room in the house, at first daring then imploring him to hit her. She was getting more drunk. Dad was getting more mad. Suddenly, Dad grabbed her by the arms, squared her shoulders to him, and then as Mom raised a hand in front of her face in a feeble attempt to block his fist, he punched her twice in the mouth. My older brother and I watched in horror and disbelief. Then, my brother, just sixteen years old at the time, placed his body between them and told our father it was time to go. That was the last night we spent together as a family.

Scenes like this one explain the childhood pact my brother and I made never to marry or become fathers ourselves. (A tacit promise that many of my clients and the other men I spoke to, who grew up with violent or abusive fathers, made to themselves.) Fifteen years later, I decided it was time to try to change this image of the four of us I'd been carrying with me all those years. I suggested family therapy. I figured even if we just sat and stared at each other for fifty minutes and then got up and left without saying a word, it would be a huge improvement. The question was, when?

The year Dana and I decided to marry presented a good excuse, as I did not want to have to think about my mother and father laying eyes on each other for the first time in almost a decade as my wife and I exchanged our vows. My father had always made clear his willingness to participate in this sort of meeting. My mother was a different story. I knew Mom's feelings about therapy. They were, if you believed her, right up there with her love for my father, the Nazis, and the GOP. To my surprise, it didn't take much to convince her.

The session itself was anticlimactic. Although she complained the whole way there, my mother seemed genuinely glad to attend. I told my parents that I was looking forward to starting a family of my own and sharing that experience with both of them, but that relations between them needed to thaw before that could happen. After about an hour and a half, Dad said he hadn't planned on staying this long but that he wanted to continue the conversation, so he was going to try to change his flight. We took a break so he could call the airline.

While we waited for Dad to finish his call, Mom told me and my therapist how ridiculous she felt this whole thing was and that she could barely stand being in the same room with him (which wasn't how it seemed when we were talking together). I remember feeling like one of those hot air balloonists who, after years of preparation, attempts to circle the world and makes it more than three quarters of the way around before suddenly crash-landing on some uncharted island in the Pacific. As Mom spoke, I felt my balloon deflate and watched my body being propelled back toward Earth.

When Dad returned, we resumed the session. My mother and father sat together on the couch. I don't know how long we'd been talking before I noticed that my mother had placed her hand on one of my father's. She just let it rest there. Eventually,

Dad noticed it, too. He took her hand in his and held it for the remainder of the session. I don't remember what else we talked about, but whatever words we exchanged wouldn't have seemed important after that.

In three beats of my heart, the session (and life) seemed to shift from bearable to beautiful. As the three of us inched forward, I watched our family's present become larger and its past smaller.

After we ended, the plan was for me to take my mother back to the airport. I was just getting ready to do so when both my parents pulled up in my father's rental car. My mother rolled down her window and said, "You don't have to bother, sweetheart, your father will give me a ride to the airport. He's headed there anyway." And then she patted his hand on the seat next to him. I kissed her through the open window. Dad opened his door, walked around the car, and gave me a huge embrace.

It's easy to underestimate the power of people sitting in a room listening to one another, but that's a lot of what good therapy is. When it comes to repairing father-son relationships and helping families heal, a little can go a long way.

The session with my mother and father not only provided me a very different memory of our last night together as a family and the kind of endings we were capable of, it cleared the way for me to have a better experience of all the endings yet to come. Prior to that, violence and addiction overshadowed everything we did. Therapy paved the way for us to create new rituals and stories, ones based on love and laughter instead of anger and bitterness. It allowed us to salvage the good stories buried under all that shame—stories of our family's bravery and heroism. Like the winter when I was a baby and burning up with fever and my father walked three miles in a blizzard to the pharmacy, wading through waist-high snowdrifts, to bring me the medicine I needed.

Stories are instruments of change. However, many of the stories we tell about our families and ourselves are what the therapist Michael White calls "problem saturated." Rather than saying good-bye to people we've lost and learning how to let go of them, according to White the work of mourning involves finding ways of "saying hullo again." When you view grief this way, therapy becomes about looking for ways of reconnecting men to their deceased fathers and helping them create rituals that honor those connections.

Connecting Rituals

Mary Pipher, therapist and author, urges people in mourning to pick something in the natural world that reminds them of their loved ones. When they see the object—the moon, the sea, a constellation, a wildflower—they can pay their respects.

In my father's last will and testament, he requested that my brother and I bury his ashes next to my dog Casper in a field belonging to a neighbor whose property abutted a farmhouse I was renting at the time. However, both my brother and I wanted Dad closer to us, somewhere we knew we would always be able to visit.

Dad's wishes were carried out, but my brother also took some of Dad's ashes and planted them in his garden while I drove a portion to Stowe, Vermont, and scattered them along Dad's favorite ski trail, a steep black diamond run called "Nose Dive." My friend Ken came with me. It was a beautiful sunny day. Blue sky as far as the eye could see. I handed Ken my poles, held the container over my head, and shushed down the trail. Now whenever I go skiing, I think of my father. He has become part of the snowcapped peaks and rushing wind when I take an exhilarating run down the mountain.

For Lenny, this sort of cosmic connection to his father did not come at the foot of a snowy trail through the woods, but rather in the smooth wooden handles of his father's masonry tools. Three years after his father died, Lenny was gathering some tools together for a stage set he was designing and building:

> I'm in my basement and I have a bucket, a big five-gallon pail that's just stuffed with all my dad's old masonry tools. And I picked up a trowel that I hadn't picked up in a couple of years, and I held it in my hand and I wept like a baby. It's just so much of him was in that, and I couldn't believe how visceral the feeling was.

Many of Lenny's earliest memories of his father revolve around his hands: the gripping of tools, the turning of nuts and screws, watching his dad working late down in the garage. His hunched-over body half swallowed by the open hood of whatever old car he was keeping on the road that year.

Lenny feels his father's presence every time he picks up one of his dad's tools. At first it was a shocking reminder of his father's death and the painful feelings surrounding his absence. Now he reaches for one of those wood-handled objects whenever he wants to feel closer to the man.

Handling his father's personal possessions released a stored association of overwhelming power for Lenny, and it invokes the Proustian distinction between voluntary and involuntary memory. Using voluntary memory, I can work my way back from an ash-covered ski trail in Stowe, Vermont, to the summer of 1974 when, after my parents' divorce, my father drove me across the country with Joel Shulman, my best friend from the eighth grade. Writing an account of our lives in this fashion, explains Sven Birkerts in his essay "Memoir and the Work of Time," brings back troves of specific information—what we ate, where we stayed, how many miles we traveled—but tells us little else about the experience.

Involuntary memory is a gateway to our real past that initiates a whole chain of associations, which eventually lead to the restoration of an entire past world. For me, an example of involuntary memory would be the hum of my father's semiautomatic Smith Corona typewriter. When you banged the keys, they made a very distinct *rat-tat-tat* sound, like a round of fireworks going off inside the house. Dad's had a shiny chrome return lever. When he came to the edge of the page, the machine would ring like an egg timer, signaling him to slap the lever to start a new line, which, as the platen made its way back across the page, sounded like one of those tin noisemakers you spin on New Year's Eve. The whole cacophony used to wake me up in the middle of the night. It was a comforting sound. Whenever I heard it, I knew my father was home, hard at work writing books or reworking his lecture notes for his morning classes, which meant he wasn't leaving us, at least not that evening.

When I went off to college, Dad upgraded to a fully automatic model and passed his old one on to me. Some of the keys were starting to stick, but most could be repaired. He had the whole machine tuned up and a new ribbon installed before giving it to me. It was one of his prized possessions, and he was profoundly disappointed that I didn't treat it the same way. But to me it was symbolic of our broken relationship. I viewed it as a sign that he didn't love me enough or was too cheap to get me a word processor or at least a newer Corona. It was stolen from the car my first day on campus.

I'd give anything to have it back now.

When I reflect on the kind of legacy as a father I'm leaving my sons, I don't just worry about ending the cycle of violence. I think about how to create new rituals that nourish and sustain us. Like the time when Julian was three and he and I were taking a bath.

This was a nightly routine, one of those special moments people tell you to cherish because "they grow up so fast." However, rarely do we heed such advice; at least not in the sleep-deprived trance in which most new parents move through their days. Instead of a daily calendar that marks important days of the month like Boxing Day and Queens Day in Canada, what I need is a datebook that offers helpful little reminders such as: "Today is the last day your son and you will ever take a 'tubby' together." Anyway, I was washing Julian's hair and asked him if he wanted to be a daddy too someday. Without skipping a beat he said, "Yes! Want to learn to type!!!"

———

My Inheritance

My father wasn't very mechanical. Changing a stylus on a turntable was undertaken with all the urgency and anxiety of an organ transplant. He didn't spend his weekends in a wood shop or outside polishing the car. He would prefer to buff up a letter of recommendation for a cherished colleague or pore over the words in one of his student's papers.

So instead of inheriting my father's power drill or hammer, I inherited his relationships. Whenever I have an occasion to see any of his former students and colleagues, I feel as if I'm in Brigadoon—the village of Scottish folklore that appears out of the clouds every hundred years—because not only does it feel like a century has passed since I saw them last, but time freezes so I never feel more than nine or ten years old when I do.

In the fall of 2002 I attended a five-year memorial lecture given in my father's honor at Princeton. At the end of the evening I went to say good-bye to Henry Levinson, a former student of Dad's who had given the talk. Henry was sitting with a group of people, holding forth and working the room the way his former professor would have. I came up behind his wheelchair (Henry has MS) and gently placed my hands on his shoulders signaling my readiness to leave and waited patiently for him to finish his conversation so we could say good-bye.

Suddenly, Henry reached up, grabbed my head, and pulled me closer to him so that my face was pressed up against his. "Jonathan, don't ever stop being you," he said. The inflection in his voice sounded so much like my father's, it sent chills up and down my spine, awakening my body from a five-year coma.

14

Prayer as a Form of Remembrance

See the dragon's beautiful yellow eyes
brightly in the sky.
The dragon's fire melts into spirit.
The dragon gently roars,
until he floats away.

—*THE OLD DRAGON* BY
JULIAN BLACKBURN DIAMOND (AGE 5)

THE NIGHT MY FATHER DIED, I discovered a prayer tucked inside the jacket sleeve of Sebastian Junger's *The Perfect Storm;* both were resting on the nightstand beside his bed. In many ways, the title of Junger's book was the perfect metaphor for my father's personality. Dad's energy, charisma, and capacity for love were as awe-inspiring as his anger and rage were apocalyptic. A day spent with him, good or bad, often left you feeling as if you had just been inside the vortex of a hurricane.

Dad loved storms. I think he must have seen in them a kindred spirit. The gale-force winds and high seas energized him. In the navy, while his fellow officers gutted them out from the safety of their quarters, he would go on deck to watch them. When we crossed the Atlantic on the SS *France* ocean liner, he did the same. I was five the first time we took this trip, and he used to take me up to the deck with him. Carrying me in his arms so he could move faster, he scaled the steep metal stairs, past the thick white chain with the bright red sign saying "Crew Members Only," so we could watch the weather from the best vantage point possible. The sound of the wind was deafening. *"Whataya think, Wus?"* he shouted. I tried to look, but the rain and sea spray stung my eyes. The danger made it both scary and exciting. While I felt safe in his arms, I wasn't too young at the time to recognize that I was standing in the presence of a force even more powerful and unpredictable than my father.

The prayer stowed inside *The Perfect Storm* was a more unusual find (it actually fell to the floor when I opened the book). It was printed on a small card, which had a picture of the Rocky Mountains and the words "God's Protection" on its cover. Inside it read:

THE LORD OUR PROTECTOR

I Look to the mountains;
    where will my help come from?
My help will come from the Lord,
    who made heaven and earth,
He will not let you fall;
    your protector is always awake.

The protector of Israel;
    never dozes or sleeps.
The Lord will guard you;
    He is by your side to protect you.
The sun will not hurt you during the day,
    nor the moon during the night.

The Lord will protect you from all danger;
　　He will keep you safe.
He will protect you as you come and go
　　now and forever.

　　　　　　　　　　　　　　—PSALM 121

Churchgoers who volunteer to visit the sick and dying give this sort of religious paraphernalia to hospital patients. Jews have their own brand of these spiritual Avon callers. Given how annoying Dad found this kind of piety, he was incredibly patient with these people.

Nevertheless, it was unlike my father to hold on to anything with the words "God's Protection" on it, especially not a psalm from something called *The Good News Bible*. What's more, I know it wasn't doubling as a bookmark, as there was already one in the book. All of this left me wondering at 2 A.M.—the hour it was revealed to me—just who the prayer's message was intended for.

An inexplicable peace came over me after I read it. Its words reminded me of an exchange I once heard between the radio interviewer Terry Gross and the jazz singer Joe Williams. Gross asked Williams about a Star of David she noticed he was wearing around his neck. He said it was a gift from his wife along with a Saint Francis of Assisi medallion with the phrase "Watch over my career" inscribed on it. When she asked him if either he or his spouse was Jewish, he laughed and replied, "No, we just don't like to take any chances."

As big a nonbeliever as my father was, it brought me great comfort knowing he wasn't taking any chances either.

Dad always said that he wasn't afraid of dying, he just didn't want to be there when it happened. He faced death with the same irreverent spirit he faced life with. Eventually, humor gave way to fear. "Dad, are you scared of dying?" I asked him during one of our visits at the hospital. "You bet!" he answered. "What are you scared of?" "You know, I fear the usual stuff—the tape, my stream of consciousness, going blank. I know that's a ridiculous thing to be afraid of, it happens every night we go to sleep. I always fantasized about becoming the world's most remembered expert on dying, like that well-known cardinal who died with such grace and dignity. You can't live unless you know how to die, but my anxieties about death are ruining my experience of dying. I had a lot of acceptance when I first found out about the cancer. I was ready for whatever life's plan was for me, but after all this time I've gotten chicken. I want to stick around."

Somewhere between the time we had that exchange and when he died, Dad found the acceptance and courage he was searching for.

After my father died, my stepmother found a note among his papers at the hospital that read: "In the hospital—again. There's no more normal for me—or rather, visits to the doctors' offices, dialysis and hospital stays are now normal for me. This is tough, cancer hacks away at you. Yet, I'm full of a sense of well-being. It's just a sense of being all right in this new world I've had to live with. It's a sense of being lifted up."

When the movie *The Perfect Storm* came out, I went to see it with my friend Prudence. As the theater lights started to dim I was transported back to that last night spent with my father. When the lights went black, I turned to Pru and whispered, "This was the last book my father read before he died." In that moment, I felt as if I was with him again. I also began to more fully understand why he would have chosen that particular book to console himself with during those final days. If there was ever a book that captured my father's personal belief about death, it was this one.

Death is not just a transcendent experience; it's a visceral one. Junger's story makes no bones about this, with an entire chapter devoted to the experience of drowning. Dad's bookmark was pressed firmly between the pages of that chapter, which opens with a quote from Revelation 6:8: "Behold a pale horse, and his name who sat on him was Death, and Hell followed with him."

Like the seamen fighting for their lives aboard the *Andrea Gail,* Dad had reached a position from which he couldn't recover. Among boat builders and mariners, this is known as the zero-moment point—the point of no return. My father wasn't reading *The Perfect Storm* for spiritual solace; he was preparing himself for death by trying to master his fear of dying.

In his classic paper "Remembering, Repeating, Working Through," Freud discusses how we remember forgotten traumas not as memories but as actions, actions we repeat but are not conscious of repeating. The telling and retelling of our stories over and over in therapy (and writing) is an attempt to remember and master traumatic experience. This, then, is the essential process of grieving—repeating again and again the images of, and feelings about, our lost loved one until the mourning process is completed. Working through is about making ourselves whole again.

Similar to Freud's observations about trauma, prayer is also a form of remembering. In mourning, we turn to prayer for solace and comfort. The healing powers of prayer, long understood and appreciated by poets, are now supported by medical research and documented in the scientific literature.

Paraphrasing Kahlil Gibran, love does not die quickly, so prayer becomes another way to celebrate the depth of the union. This book is my remembrance. Its pages, like my tears, are sad but glistening with the beauty of the past.

I miss you, Dad.

Epilogue

When a father gives to his son, both laugh; when a son gives to his father, both cry.

—YIDDISH PROVERB

WRITING THIS BOOK, I hoped to go out in a blaze of foliage. My publisher granted me a two-month extension to October 24. How much of a man's life can you fit into a book about his death if you only have eight weeks left to write it in? I remember panicking about it at the time. But then that deadline came and went. So I had to reconcile myself to the book coming out of the oven like a Thanksgiving turkey. No go. Would you believe another Hanukkah miracle? Uh-uh. A Christmas story? Not Dad's style. December 27, his memorial day? I was sure that would be it, but like the actual day itself, it was a little anticlimactic. No big finish.

By this time my son Julian was asking me every day—morning, noon, and night—"Daddy, are you done yet?" I promised him that when the time came, he could type the book's last words.

On Monday morning January 5, 2004, at 6:30 A.M., Julian was the first one up. He came downstairs rubbing the sleep from his eyes and asked me again, "Daddy, are you done yet?" This time I said, "As a matter of fact, we're there!" Julian crawled into my lap. I was just going to have him type "The end." But my son has a mind like a steel trap. I knew that whenever the book came back from the printer, the first thing he would do is ask me, "Where are the words I typed?" So I deleted the book's last sentence and watched him type it again:

"I m-i-s-s y-o-u, D-a-d."

Acknowledgments

Many people "sat shiva" with me during the writing of this book and have helped give it shape and form. In fact, I have been fortunate to receive significant amounts of feedback from numerous readers—brilliant writers and thinkers all—who wisely advised me to cut, change, alter, punctuate, rewrite, revise, redo, rethink, rework, tweak, turn a phrase, write with more authority ("You're the expert"), decenter yourself ("Just tell your story"), use a more intimate voice, take a more distant tone, throw out the first three chapters, throw out the last three chapters, start over, get a grip, dream on, take a stiff drink, get a life, and gently asked the tough, probing questions such as: "You're not going to put that in print, are you!?!" or "I hope you know the name of a good litigator." Much of what is good about the book came from them. The faults I claim as my own. However, if you want to know where they originated from, here is a list of names: Doug Anderson, Chris Behan, Steve Berman, Calvin Carr, Jan Carr, Carol Edelstein, Ken Epstein, Jean Footit, Prudence Grand, Meryl Joseph, Francesca Kelly, Henry Levinson, Jean Lightfoot, Lorena Loubsky-Lonnerghan, Ann McNelly, Samuel Muri, Margaret

O'Connor, Janine Roberts, Bill Ryan, Marion Sandmier, Peggy Sax, Gerry Schamess, Shanti Shapiro, Pam Smith, Barry Sparks, Carol Stowe, Martha Sweezy, Melissa Tefft (who left me the single best voice mail a writer has ever received), Rabbi Sheila Peltz Weinberg, Genie Zeiger, and Rob Zucker. A special thanks to Lois Shawver (who is solely responsible for fixing the gross errors in my reading of Wittgenstein) and the rest of my PMTH pals who walked with me along the way—Ester de Beer, Helen Douglas, Lynn Hoffman, Katherine Levine, Val Lewis, Kiernan O'Rourke-Phipps, Joe Pfeiffer, Karen Ray, Brent Dean Robbins, Len Schwartzburd, Jerry Shaffer, Karin Taverniers, and Judy Weintraub. And a heartfelt embrace for Elliott Smolensky and Lenny Weeks, who kept me smiling and rolling (when the royalties were not), and my friends Arlene, Beth, Connie, Eileen, Kim, Maria, Marilyn, Mike and Nancy of McCuskers on the Buckland side of Shelburne Falls—the only literary marketplace worth its salt!

Like a gathering of enthusiastic mourners at a dead man's wake, no group expressed more joy (and relief) when the book made its final journey into print than my editor Tom Miller and the talented staff at John Wiley & Sons. A special shout-out to Teryn Kendall, who served as midwife to the book. Her vision and guidance came at a crucial time and gave me the confidence to see the project through to completion. I thank them all for their patience.

I chose my agent, Susan Lee Cohen, because the authors she represents keep writing better and better books and with every volume find more and more gushing things to say about her in their acknowledgments. I now understand why, and I am blessed to add my voice to theirs.

Large portions of the manuscript were completed at the Vermont home of Ann and Richard Barnet. Dick was one of my intellectual heroes. I read all his books in college, including his tour de force *Global Reach*—the first book to expose the increasing power and expansion of multinational corporations for the siren songs they truly are—while his best work, his son Michael (the third in a trilogy), sat next to me in class. Dick's impressive corpus demonstrates what Judaism calls "the ability to look down on the sky." After sitting at his desk in Ryegate, I have a much better understanding of how he came by this view. I'm grateful. Dick died on December 23, 2004. With his passing the world doesn't seem as safe a place, and another precious part of our global community seems broken and in need of repair. The good news is that the collection of writing he left behind provides us the blueprint for fixing it. I pray we have the courage and wisdom to follow it.

To Barbara Cheresh for her many acts of grace and for sharing her sanctuary in Provincetown with a lesser artist.

I'm always grateful for the love and support of my relatives (especially the ones who are still talking to me): Jennifer, Jamie, Beth, Scott, Boo, E.J., Judy, Jojo, Ray, Doug, Lauren, Amy Lynn, Kimberly, Joyce, and Moose.

To my uncle Ted—who was there for his brother when he needed him most; and Denise, who knows all too well what this book is about; and my own brother, Michael, hoping it helps him find his way back to me.

Another writer I admire carries inside her eyeglass case a small piece of paper with the following words printed on it: "Friends are God's way of saying 'I'm sorry.'" Here are some of the best apologies I've received to date: James, Andrea, Pan, Paul, Diane, Cal, and Jan.

To the fathers: "News," Deano, Jon, Ken, Jeff, Chris, Rob, and their families: Esa, Joey, Johanna, Mary Jo, Mya, Jesse, Karen, Jacob, Leah, Ann, Hannah, Silvia, Henry, Amelia, James, Eva, Laurie, Charlie, Alice, Henry, Rachel, Benjamin, Nicholas, Mooph, and Theo—whose loving hearts and generous spirits are all the religion a person could possibly need.

To my beloveds Boo, Caryn, Dusty, Roget, and Pru. John Berryman said, "The artist is extremely lucky who is presented with the worst possible ordeal which will not actually kill him. At that point, he's in business." I couldn't have faced the business of writing this book without the five of you by my side.

And to my mother, Barbara Reingold Diamond, the bravest person I know.

Every serious journey or trek needs a strong guide. I am fortunate to have had many. The clients and other men and women I've chosen to write about in this book are people I admire. I've tried to write about both their strengths and their flaws, but in no way should my doing so be interpreted as my passing judgment. Put another way, I respect and love them all.

A project of this kind is an enormous undertaking requiring great patience and perseverance. I tried to meet this challenge with all the grace and poise I could muster; however, I knew I was in trouble when the "sell by" date on the milk carton in the refrigerator started flashing my deadline. When this happened, my wife, Dana, stepped up to the plate. As I toiled away writing the book's final chapters, she performed her duties as book widow, primary breadwinner, and parent with unsurpassed love and generosity, providing my sons, Julian and Oliver, and the other wildlife that make our house their home with the additional TLC needed to get all of us through this stressful period. She is the only person who has suffered more than I have during the writing of this book, and as a result will, no doubt, be the only person to receive fewer rewards for her efforts.

For Dana, broke again; I only know the stay of your secure, firm embrace—love follows, pen in hand.

Notes

PREFACE

xii *At times, mourning requires* Hans Loewald, *Papers on Psychoanalysis* (New Haven, CT: Yale University Press, 1980).

xiii *There is an Aboriginal creation myth* Bruce Chatwin, *The Songlines.* (New York: Viking Press, 1987), p. 2.

xiv *"endure the separation of death, the affliction of mourning"* David and Judy Ray (eds.), *Fathers, A Collection of Poems* (New York: St Martin's Press, 1997), p. xvi.

INTRODUCTION

8 *"little alleluias"* Mary Oliver, *Long Life: Essays and Other Writing* (Cambridge, MA: DaCapo Press, 2004), p. xiv.

1. HOW MEN GRIEVE

14 *The most well known of this type of approach* Elisabeth Kübler-Ross, *On Death and Dying* (New York: Macmillan, 1969).

15 *"The last time I was privileged to shake my father's hand"* Carroll Stowe, "The Way It Is in the Country," in *Selections from 25 Years of the* Heath Herald (Greenfield, MA: Staples, 2004), p. 5.

15 *"We're an impatient culture"* Hope Edelman, *Motherless Daughters: The Legacy of Loss* (Weston, MA: Addison-Wesley, 1994), pp. 5–6.

15 *"If it takes nine months"* Hope Edelman, *Motherless Daughters* (Weston, MA: Addison-Wesley, 1994), p. 6.

16 *"All my ideas and concepts"* Author, educator, and therapist Katherine Levine first passed this advice on to me. I'm grateful for her permission to recycle it here.

17 *It is up to therapist* When having dialogues of such gravity and importance, professionals need to maintain what I, borrowing philosopher Martin Buber's term, call an "uncertain certainty," or what some in my field refer to as a "non expert" or "not knowing" style of address. For further discussion, see Lynn Hoffman, *Family Therapy: An Intimate History* (New York: W.W. Norton, 2002); and Harlene Anderson and Harold Goolishian, "The Client Is the Expert: A Not Knowing Approach to Therapy," in *Therapy as Social Construction*, K. Gergen and S. McNamee (eds.) (Newbury Park, CA: Sage Publications, 1992), pp. 25–39.

18 *"compounded by attributions"* Louise Kaplan, *No Voice Is Ever Wholly Lost* (New York: Simon & Schuster, 1995), pp. 53–54.

20 *To one degree* Mark Epstein, *Going to Pieces without Falling Apart: A Buddhist Perspective on Wholeness* (New York: Broadway Books, 1998), p. 63.

21 *the man who lost his father* Louise Kaplan, *No Voice Is Ever Wholly Lost* (New York: Simon & Schuster, 1995).

22 *The heart can open* Mark Epstein, *Going to Pieces without Falling Apart: A Buddhist Perspective on Wholeness* (New York: Broadway Books, 1998), p. 64.

22 *the way Doris Lessing describes* "What Good Times We All Had Then," in *Fathers: Reflections by Daughters*, Ursula Owen (ed.) (New York: Pantheon Books, 1983), pp. 65–75.

2. DO YOU KNOW WHY YOU'RE WONDERFUL?

27 *"Hints and guesses"* T. S. Eliot, *The Four Quartets* (New York: Harcourt Brace Jovanovich, 1943), p. 136.

28 *"You will see not only"* Eckhart Tolle, *Stillness Speaks* (Vancouver: Namaste Publishing, 2003), p. 103.

36 *"a gutsy life-affirming response"* Janis Abrahm Spring, *How Can I Forgive You? The Courage to Forgive, The Freedom Not To* (New York: HarperCollins, 2004), p. 53.

36 *apart from the offense* When someone willfully and maliciously hurts you, forgiveness is an option, not a requirement. You can recover from interpersonal and emotional injury with or without forgiveness. When it's earned, forgiveness can be rewarding for both the injured and offending party; but you can make peace with yourself and what happened to you with or without forgiving the person who hurt you. And you can do this for yourself, as Spring writes, "Even if the offender is unapologetic, even if he refuses to acknowledge your pain or apply a drop of salve to your wound—*even if he has passed on*" [my emphasis added]. Janis Abrahm Spring, *How Can I Forgive You? The*

Courage to Forgive, The Freedom Not To (New York: HarperCollins, 2004), p. 3.

40 *My father and my five-and-a-half-month-old son* Paul Zweig, "Departures," in Maura Spiegel and Richard Tristman (eds.), *The Grim Reader: Writings on Death, Dying, and Living On* (New York: Anchor Books, 1997), p. 47.

3. HELP ME TO REMEMBER YOU

44 *"Boys who grow up estranged from their fathers"* Jon Katz, *Running to the Mountain* (New York: Broadway Books, 1999), p. 29.

44 *"don't know how to do a lot of things"* Jon Katz, *Running to the Mountain* (New York: Broadway Books, 1999), pp. 29–30.

49 *"If psychoanalysis is the impossible profession"* Andrew Solomon, *The Noonday Demon: An Atlas of Depression* (New York: Simon & Schuster, 2001), p. 246.

51 *"Welcome this pain"* The quotation from Ovid I have taken from Andrew Solomon's *The Noonday Demon: An Atlas of Depression* (New York: Simon & Schuster, 2001), p. 38.

51 *"Pain is inevitable"* The original source of this quote was R. D. Laing, who wrote, "There is a great deal of pain in life and perhaps the only pain that can be avoided is the pain that comes from trying to avoid pain." Personally, I like Roget's version better.

52 *"Grief is depression in proportion"* Andrew Solomon, *The Noonday Demon: An Atlas of Depression* (New York: Simon & Schuster, 2001), p. 16.

53 *men rely on activity* Tom Golden, *Swallowed by a Snake: The Gift of the Masculine Side of Healing* (Gaithersburg, MD: Golden Healing Publishing, 1996/2000), pp. 135–136.

54 *"When it comes to our societal understanding of grief"* Elizabeth DeVita-Raeburn, *The Empty Room* (New York: Scribner, 2004), p. 184.

4. THERE'S NO PLACE LIKE HOME

70 *"I imagine one reason"* James Baldwin in Janis Abrahm Spring, *How Can I Forgive You?* (New York: HarperCollins, 2004), p. 56.

71 *"Too often what fathers bequeath"* Terry Real, *I Don't Want to Talk about It: Overcoming the Secret Legacy of Male Depression* (New York: Simon & Schuster, 1997), p. 236.

75 *"For me there would be"* Simon Wiesenthal, *The Sunflower: On the Possibilities and Limits of Forgiveness* (New York: Schocken Books, 1998), p. 15.

77 *"The capacity to love"* Stephen Mitchell, *Can Love Last? The Fate of Romance Over Time* (New York: W.W. Norton, 2002), p. 144.

80 *When mourning* Mark Doty, *Heaven's Coast: A Memoir* (New York: HarperCollins, 1996), p. 287.

5. HOW DEEP IS THE WELL?

95 *"That we can grieve"* Andrea Hairston, personal communication, 2005.

6. THE WISHING WELL

108 *In Miller's modern American classic* Arthur Miller, *Death of a Salesman* (New York: Viking Press, 1958/1949).

7. WITTGENSTEIN'S TIGERS

118 *One day my father* Malcolm Diamond, *Martin Buber: Jewish Existentialist* (Oxford, England: Oxford University Press, 1960), p. 207.

123 *Christopher Bollas's term* Christopher Bollas, *Cracking Up: The Work of Unconscious Experience* (New York: Hill & Wang, 1995), p. 7.

126 *Recently, I read a passage* The student was Wasfi Hjab. His story is recounted in David Edmonds and John Eidinow's *Wittgenstein's Poker* (New York: HarperCollins, 2001), pp. 10–11.

126 *"It is clear great flyers"* Sam Keen, *Learning to Fly* (New York: Broadway Books, 1999), p. 119.

8. WHAT WAS HE THINKING!?!

133 *become a great nation* The philosopher Søren Kierkegaard also wished to be present at the time when Abraham lifted up his eyes and saw Mount Moriah far off and went alone with Isaac up the mountain. Kirkegaard's imagining was the subject of his *Fear and Trembling* (Princeton, NJ: Princeton University Press, 1941/1954).

133 *his father's death* Another retelling of the story of Abraham and Isaac I was drawn to is found in Bruce Feiler's *Abraham: A Journey to the Heart of Three Faiths* (New York: William & Morrow, 2002). For all the differences in how Jews, Christians, and Muslims interpret the story of the offering, for Feiler the deeper revelation is how all three religions have chosen to place the narrative of a father preparing to kill his son at the heart of their self-understanding.

Another measure of this dark commonality the three share is a legend surrounding the offering. According to Feiler (p. 109), what happens to Isaac after the angel of mercy delivers God's message to Abraham is when the narrative becomes more a story about a son saving his father rather than a father (or *the* Father) rescuing one of his children:

> Immediately after the boy is saved, he lies on the altar clutching the knife; the emotion of the ordeal flooding his body, God tells him he will grant him any prayer. "O God, I pray that you grant me this," the boy says. "When any person in any era meets you at the gates of Heaven—whether they believe in you or not—I ask that you allow them to enter Paradise."

Faced with the phantom of his own elimination, Abraham's son responds with a Call of his own. He asks God to bless those who bless God, and bless those who curse him. The comprehensive blessing God granted to Abraham is now returned as an even greater request from Abraham's son. Violence, in other words, can turn to virtue in an instant.

And that is exactly what Isaac did. He transformed the most horrible act a father could perpetrate upon a son into the father's greatest moment of triumph and salvation. In my book, it is Isaac who moves closer to God as a result of what transpired on the Mount. Not only because he was able to love his father and ensure Abraham's place in heaven, even though his father was willing to murder him; but because of his commitment to seeing that no father or son is ever put in that position again.

140   *Therapists are purveyors of hope*   For further discussion of therapy as a hopeful rather than a pathologizing endeavor, see Mary Pipher, *The Shelter of Each Other: Rebuilding Our Families* (New York: Ballantine Books, 1996), pp. 134–153; and Michael White and David Epston, *Narrative Means to Therapeutic Ends* (New York: W.W. Norton, 1990).

140   *"relational heroes"*   Terry Real, *I Don't Want to Talk about It: Overcoming the Secret Legacy of Male Depression* (New York: Simon & Schuster, 1997), p. 230.

9. MOM

148   *the larger culture*   Bob Blauner (ed.), *Our Mothers' Spirits: Great Writers on the Death of Mothers and the Grief of Men* (New York: Regan Books, 1998), pp. 245–246.

155   *the annulment of vows*   Rabbi David Cooper, *God Is a Verb* (New York: Riverhead Books, 1997), p. 255.

156   *another Jewish ritual*   Rabbi David Cooper, *God Is a Verb* (New York: Riverhead Books, 1997), p. 256.

157   *"And did you get what"*   Raymond Carver, "Late Fragment," in Neil Astley (ed.), *Staying Alive: Real Poems for Unreal Times* (New York: Miramax Books, 2003), p. 456.

160   *"I wanted the images"*   Paul Auster, *Invention of Solitude* (New York: Penguin, 1982), p. 14.

10. "IS THIS WHAT I WANT TO DO WITH MY DEATH?"

165   *"We hide death"*   Marie De Hennezel, *Intimate Death: How the Dying Teach Us How to Live* (New York: Vintage Books, 1997), p. xi.

165   *"In Western society"*   Rob Zucker, "Honor and Conflict: David Zinner Discusses the Sacred Art of Jewish Bereavement," from *The Grief and Healing Newsletter*, Spring 2004, pp. 1–2. Rob Zucker is a grief

counselor and publisher of *The Grief and Healing Newsletter* (www.griefandhealingnewsletter.com).

173   *At the onset of his illness*   Sherwin Nuland, *How We Die: Reflections on Life's Final Chapter* (New York: Vintage Books, 1993), p. 257.

175   *Pia Melody called these*   I am relying on Terry Real's discussion of Melody's work in his *I Don't Want to Talk about It: Overcoming the Secret Legacy of Male Depression* (New York: Simon & Schuster, 1997), p. 206.

177   *"technological panoply"*   Sherwin Nuland, *How We Die: Reflections on Life's Final Chapter* (New York: Vintage Books, 1993), p. 254.

178   *"In the name of Hippocrates"*   Sherwin Nuland, *How We Die: Reflections on Life's Final Chapter* (New York: Vintage Books, 1993).

178   *"I couldn't take away his only hope"*   For a more in-depth discussion of hope and the cancer patient—and the medical community's relation to both, see Sherwin Nuland, *How We Die: Reflections on Life's Final Chapter* (New York: Vintage Books, 1993), pp. 223–241.

11. THE SERENITY PRAYER

187   *"Look, somebody wonderful lived"*   E. M. Broner, *Mornings and Mourning: A Kaddish Journal* (New York: HarperCollins, 1994), p. 1.

187   *"Young I think"*   E. M. Broner, *Mornings and Mourning: A Kaddish Journal* (New York: HarperCollins, 1994), pp. 6–7.

190   *"As a five year old"*   Malcolm Diamond, *House-Breaking the Ego: The Self and World Religions* (unpublished manuscript).

191   *"prayer of action"*   Richard Foster, *Prayer: Finding the Heart's True Home* (San Francisco: HarperSanFrancisco, 1992), p. 9.

192   *"it is hard to be"*   Julia Cameron, *The Sound of Paper: Starting from Scratch* (New York: Jeremy Tarcher/Penguin, 2004), p. 34.

192   *"Much of life"*   Naomi Rachel Remen, *Kitchen Table Wisdom: Stories That Heal* (New York: Riverhead Books, 1996), p. 301.

195   *"there are circumstances"*   Elisabeth Sifton, *The Serenity Prayer: Faith and Politics in Times of Peace and War* (New York: W.W. Norton, 2003), p. 293.

197   *"Each of us was in your life"*   Mitch Albom, *The Five People You Meet in Heaven* (New York: Hyperion, 2003), p. 1.

198   *Like my father*   Tikkun means "repair" or "amend" and refers to a notion written about in the Kabbalah, a body of Jewish mystical teachings. According to the Kabbalah, the world was perfect once and was contained within perfect spheres. Somehow, the spheres broke, and the ethers within them escaped. The world as we know it has scattered throughout these shards of broken glass and these escaped ethers. Over time, different Jewish religious groups have proffered different strategies for effecting the Tikkun, or repair, of the world—of returning the world to its mythical, prior, perfect condition.

198   *"Nothing worth doing"* Elisabeth Sifton, *The Serenity Prayer: Faith and Politics in Times of Peace and War* (New York: W.W. Norton, 2003), p. 349.

12. PARTING WORDS

204   *one can witness* Bernie Siegel, Foreword in Paul Roud, *Making Miracles* (New York: Warner Books, 1990), pp. xii–xiii.

211   *"like bitch-slapping E.T."* Anne Lamott, *Traveling Mercies: Some Thoughts on Faith* (New York: Anchor Books, 2000), p. 93.

13. FATHERING WITHOUT FATHERS

214   *"Our lives are shaped"* Hope Edelman, *Motherless Daughters: The Legacy of Loss* (Weston, MA: Addison-Wesley, 1994), p. 283.

214   *In a radio interview* This story is recounted in Dan Kindlor's and Michael Thompson's *Raising Cain: Protecting the Emotional Life of Boys* (New York: Ballantine Books, 2000), p. 97.

217   *Longitudinal studies show* William Pollack, *Real Boys: Rescuing Our Sons from the Myths of Boyhood* (New York: Henry Holt, 1998), pp. 113–144.

217   *"Fathers are doing more fathering"* Grace Paley, "Fathers," poem in *The New Yorker*, June 17 and 24, 2002.

219   *Many fathers fear* William Pollack, *Real Boys: Rescuing Our Sons from the Myths of Boyhood* (New York: Henry Holt, 1998), p. 128.

219   *Therapy is a meaning-building activity* Mary Pipher, *The Shelter of Each Other: Rebuilding Our Families* (New York: Ballantine Books, 1996), p. 139.

223   *the work of mourning* Michael White, "Saying Hullo Again" in *Selected Papers* (Adelaide, Australia: Dulwich Centre Publications, 1989), pp. 29–36.

223   *pick something in the natural world* Mary Pipher, *The Shelter of Each Other: Rebuilding Our Families* (New York: Ballantine Books, 1996), p. 243.

224   *brings back troves* Sven Birkerts, "Memoir and the Work of Time" in *Poets and Writers*, Vol. 33, No. 3 (2005), pp. 21–26.

14. PRAYER AS A FORM OF REMEMBRANCE

233   *"Behold a pale horse"* This passage from Revelation is quoted in Sebastian Junger, *The Perfect Storm* (New York: W.W. Norton, 1997), p. 136.

233   *In his classic paper* Sigmund Freud, "Remembering, Repeating, Working Through," in J. Strachey (ed. & trans.) *The Standard Edition of the Complete Psychological Works of Sigmund Freud* (Vol. 12), (London: Hogarth Press, 1958) (Original work published 1914), p. 155.

233   *love does not die quickly* Kahlil Gibran, *The Prophet* (New York: Knopf, 1923).

Recommended Reading

Chetnick, Neil. *Fatherloss: How Sons of All Ages Come to Terms with the Death of Their Dads.* New York: Hyperion, 2001.

Conroy, Pat. *My Losing Season.* New York: Doubleday, 2002.

De Hennezel, Marie. *Intimate Death: How the Dying Teach Us How to Live.* New York: Vintage Books, 1997.

Didion, Joan. *The Year of Magical Thinking.* New York: Alfred A. Knopf, 2005.

Doty, Mark. *Heaven's Coast.* New York: HarperCollins, 1996.

Edelman, Hope. *Motherless Daughters: The Legacy of Loss.* Weston, MA: Addison-Wesley, 1994.

Epstein, Mark. *Going to Pieces without Falling Apart: A Buddhist Perspective on Wholeness.* New York: Broadway Books, 1998.

Fisher, Antoine Quenton. *Finding Fish.* New York: Perennial, 2001.

Golden, Tom. *Swallowed by a Snake: The Gift of the Masculine Side of Healing.* Gaithersburg, MD: Golden Healing Publishing, 2000.

Goldman, Ari. *Living a Year of Kaddish.* New York: Schocken Books, 2003.

Hamill, Pete. *A Drinking Life.* New York: Little, Brown and Company, 1994.

Kaplan, Louise. *No Voice Is Ever Wholly Lost.* New York: Simon & Schuster, 1995.

Katz, Jon. *Running to the Mountain.* New York: Broadway Books, 1999.

Lamott, Anne. *Traveling Mercies: Some Thoughts on Faith.* New York: Anchor Books, 2000.

McEnroe, Collin. *My Father's Footprints.* New York: Warner Books, 2003.

Nhat Hanh, Thich. *Anger.* New York: Riverhead Books, 2001.

Nuland, Sherwin. *How We Die: Reflections on Life's Final Chapter.* New York: Vintage Books, 1995.

Olds, Sharon. *The Father.* New York: Alfred A. Knopf, 1999.

Ray, David, and Judy Ray (eds.). *Fathers: A Collection of Poems.* New York: St. Martin's Griffin Press, 1997.

Real, Terry. *I Don't Want to Talk about It: Overcoming the Secret Legacy of Male Depression.* New York: Simon & Schuster, 1997.

Romanyshyn, Robert. *The Soul in Grief: Love, Death and Transformation.* Berkeley CA: North Atlantic Books, 1999.

Ryan, William P. *The Bench, the Council, and the Prayer.* Ashfield, MA: Temenos Press, 2002.

Solomon, Andrew. *The Noonday Demon: An Atlas of Depression.* New York: Simon & Schuster, 2001.

Stowe, Carroll. *"The Way It Is in the Country": Selections from 25 Years of the* Heath Herald. (Write to: The *Heath Herald*, Heath, MA 01346).

Wideman, John Edgar. *Fatheralong: Mediations on Fathers and Sons, Race and Society.* New York: Pantheon Books, 1994.

Wieseltier, Leon. *Kaddish.* New York: Alfred A. Knopf, 1998.

Index

abandonment, 41–44
  acceptance and, 51–55
  depression and, 46–48
  Ebbets Field (Jonathan
    Diamond), 66–68
  forgiveness and, 75–77
  impact on men, 44–46
  reconciliation and, 55–65
  shamelessness and, 175
  suicide as, 48–51
Abraham-Isaac story, 131–134
abuse
  child, 134–139
  spouse, 7, 205–209
  See also alcoholism; anger
acceptance, 27–29
  grieving and, 37–38, 231–232
  of impending death, 29–36,
    109–113
  pain and, 51–55
  suicide and, 49–50
  Thanksgiving '97 (Jonathan
    Diamond), 39–40
  unconditional love and, 32–34

addiction. *See* alcoholism, substance abuse
Al-Anon, 194. *See also* alcoholism
Albom, Mitch, 197
Alcoholics Anonymous (AA), 93,
  193. *See also* alcoholism
alcoholism, 149
  acceptance and, 34–36
  recovery from, 191
  See also substance abuse
Allen, Woody, 117
"Amazing Grace" (hymn), 203–204
anger
  as acceptable male emotion, 70
  forgiveness and, 70–77
  as inherited trait, 210–211
  Piano Lesson (Jonathan Dia-
    mond), 81–82
  resentment toward surviving
    parent, 151–155
  shame and, 78–80
  "trading places" question and,
    92–93
  See also redemption